AF255449

The Poetics of Matthew 1

The Poetics of Matthew 1

— The Five References to Mothers and Other Patterns —

Timothy Lewis

RESOURCE *Publications* · Eugene, Oregon

THE POETICS OF MATTHEW 1
The Five References to Mothers and Other Patterns

Resource Publications
An Imprint of Wipf and Stock Publishers
199 W. 8th Ave., Suite 3
Eugene, OR 97401

www.wipfandstock.com

PAPERBACK ISBN: 978-1-6667-6483-3
HARDCOVER ISBN: 978-1-6667-6484-0
EBOOK ISBN: 978-1-6667-6485-7

01/03/23

Contents

Figures

Introduction

THE FIRST CHAPTER OF Matthew invites a comparison of five paternities when it refers to particular fathers acquiring particular heirs from particular mothers among the forty "progenerations" of heirs in the Messiah's lineage. In verses 3, 5, 6, and 16, five heir productions are highlighted with references to mothers:

> Judah produced Perez and Zerah *from Tamar* . . . Salmon produced Boaz *from Rahab,* Boaz produced Obed *from Ruth* . . . David produced Solomon *from her of Uriah* . . . Jesus (called Messiah) was produced *from Mary* whose husband was Joseph.[1]

Seeing as *all* heirs, in reality, have been born from mothers, there must be a reason for highlighting only particular cases in which the heirs of five fathers are said to have been produced from five mothers.

Numerous theories have arisen to explain the references to mothers in the Messiah's genealogy. Rarely do commentators think that the point is to compare anything other than the mothers themselves.[2] Back in 2000, Warren Carter included six different interpretations in his commentary on Matthew, all of which compared the women and their respective circumstances.[3]

---

1. Ἰούδας δὲ ἐγέννησεν τὸν Φαρὲς καὶ τὸν Ζάρα ἐκ τῆς Θαμάρ . . . Σαλμὼν δὲ ἐγέννησεν τὸν Βόες ἐκ τῆς Ῥαχάβ, Βόες δὲ ἐγέννησεν τὸν Ἰωβὴδ ἐκ τῆς Ῥούθ . . . Δαυὶδ δὲ ἐγέννησεν τὸν Σολομῶνα ἐκ τῆς τοῦ Οὐρίου . . . Ἰωσὴφ τὸν ἄνδρα Μαρίας, ἐξ ἧς ἐγεννήθη Ἰησοῦς ὁ λεγόμενος χριστός. The text cited is Holmes, *Greek New Testament,* abbreviated hereafter as "SBLGNT." Bible translations are my own.

2. Evans, "'Book of the Genesis,'" 70, thought to compare the *heirs* rather than the mothers ("the focus may not be so much on the four/five women, but on their respective offspring"). But later, in his 2012 commentary, he reverts to the common practice of comparing the mothers. Evans, *Matthew,* 35–36.

3. Carter, *Matthew and the Margins,* 59–61.

Between 2011 and 2014 three books appeared on the topic of the mothers in the Messiah's genealogy in which three more interpretations were proposed (by Jason B. Hood, Amy E. Richter, and E. Anne Clements).[4] Hood saw a Gentile pattern when comparing Tamar, Rahab, Ruth, and Uriah. Richter saw a redemptive pattern based on the kind of sins associated with all the women (and originating from the legend of the wayward angels as depicted in Enochic literature). Clements saw a subversion of patriarchal structures which questioned the exercise of patriarchy and lineage for constituting the new messianic people of God. None of these studies compared the respective paternities of the highlighted fathers who, according to the text, are the ones who procured their heirs from five mothers (passively in the case of Joseph according to verse 16).

When I first became interested in the topic in 2016, I felt I was living in the golden age of interpretations for this unsolved mystery. I excitedly consulted every journal article I could find on the topic. But despite the multiplicity of theories for the references to mothers, I could not find any studies comparing the five fathers.

I managed to find a few sentences by scholars who very briefly thought to compare the five fathers. Amy Jill-Levine's page of comments offered the most sustained attempt to identify a potential pattern among the five fathers.[5]

I was thrilled when, in 2019, a more in-depth attempt to compare the fathers was made by Sébastien Doane who wrote a journal article comparing the highlighted men by comparing their masculinities from the perspective of masculinity studies (he found "a reversal of the values associated with masculinity").[6] However, Doane's article did not study the assumed process of how each man gained his status of paternity in this elite messianic pedigree according how the five men are presented in Matthew 1.

By this time, I had given up looking for the answer in the secondary literature. I excitedly began looking for, and finding, the answer within Matthew 1, identifying various patterns on display within the text itself. Once the pattern with the fathers is seen, we will probably all wonder why we had not noticed it before.

---

4. Hood, *The Messiah, His Brothers*; Richter, *Enoch and the Gospel*; Clements, *Mothers on the Margin?*

5. Levine, "Women's Humor," 121–22.

6. Doane, "Masculinities of the Husbands," 92.

One reason for the widespread compulsion to compare the mothers is that many commentators feel there is already an excessive amount of material and commentary focusing on men in biblical texts and so it would be better to take the opportunity to focus on the women. Understandably, most feminist commentary on Matthew 1 focuses on the mothers so as to subvert the patriarchal tone of the text. Modern readers might not know what else to do about the apparent patriarchal interests at work in Matthew 1 other than to avoid the topic. Many of us might think that by *not* comparing the fathers we are resisting the patriarchal tendencies within the text and thereby preventing the perpetuation of the text's own patriarchal patterns and agendas.

It turns out, however, that if we compare the fathers, as is invited by Matthew 1, we will discover something extraordinary. The purpose of Matthew 1 is seen to be exposing patriarchy to a critique, somewhat like an ancient study in masculinity or narrative ethics. *The Poetics of Matthew 1* demonstrates this by studying various patterns at work in Matthew 1.

The present method began to emerge, fortuitously, in part from my own misunderstandings of reading R. T. France, Krister Stendahl, and Elaine Wainwright. I remember thinking that France had suggested that Matt 1:18–25 is more connected with what follows (namely Matthew 2) than to what precedes (Matt 1:1–17). Going back over France's commentary, I cannot now find any such comment. Nevertheless, this misunderstanding is what initially spurred me to want to study the interconnectedness of the first two units of Matthew.

This led me to concur with Krister Stendahl's comment that "the whole of chapter 1 has its own integrity" since the genealogy "points to what follows in 1:18–25."[7] Fortunately, I had also misunderstood Stendahl when he described Matt 1:18–25 as a large footnote explaining the end of the genealogy in verse 16 as though he meant that verses 18–25 explain the *entire* genealogy, not just verse 16. Misreading Stendahl this way, it soon became evident that both units do indeed function interdependently, cross-referencing each other. Much of verses 18–25 either continues or completes what is in verses 2–16. I began to wonder not only if there was a way to understand the two units in Matthew 1 in light of each other but that every sentence might be interpreted according to the text of Matthew 1 without relying on other references not mentioned in Matthew 1.

7. Stendahl, "Quis et Unde," 76

My third fortunate misunderstanding concerned how Elaine Wainwright had, allegedly, interpreted the references to five mothers in the Messiah's genealogy. According to Colleen Conway's summary statement, Wainwright "reads the women's anomalous presence as a threat or challenge to patriarchy . . . [but] it is doubtful that an ancient reader would understand Matthew's genealogy as a strike against patriarchy."[8] Like Conway, I imagined that Wainwright interpreted Matthew 1 as a critique of patriarchy. Unlike Conway, I began finding evidence in the text to support Wainwright's "idea," even though this was not exactly what Wainwright was saying.

After rereading Wainwright, I soon realized that she was not suggesting that the first chapter of Matthew was *purposefully* written to critique patriarchal structures but that this is a reading strategy for those of us who might take the opportunity to read the text that way. Fortunately, it was too late, as I was already finding patterns in the text indicative of such a critique. As a result, it can now be demonstrated that an ancient reader *would* be expected to understand Matthew's genealogy as a strike against patriarchy.

This is what led me to study how the patterns work within Matthew 1, enabling answers to be found for questions previously not thought to be answered within the text. The question of why there are references to mothers in the Messiah's lineage is one such question and perhaps the most perplexing for scholars.[9]

Another significant factor that led to the current book was the struggle to make sense of what verse 19 says about Joseph's initial response to Mary's pregnancy. Joseph's plans are said to be those of a "righteous one" or "right-acting man" (δίκαιος). Joseph tries to refuse Mary privately and is privately intercepted by an angel. What is the point of telling us about Joseph's initial response if he was *not* right but labeling him as being "right" (δίκαιος)?

What Joseph may have been thinking (and why Joseph is motivated to reject Mary) are issues that have not previously been resolved according to what *is* in the text. It is assumed in the commentaries that Joseph

8. Conway, *Behold the Man*, 109.

9. Anderson, for example, says, "No answer is provided in the text." Anderson, *Matthew's Narrative Web*, 51. France says, "[Matthew] gives us no overt indication . . . we cannot go beyond conjecture." France, *The Gospel of Matthew*, 38. According to Remaud, "The genealogy . . . lists four women whose presence in this succession of predominantly male generations cannot be explained satisfactorily only by biblical data." Remaud, "Les femmes dans la généalogie," 3.

is presented as thinking the wrong thing about Mary's conception leaving him unsure about what he should now do. His decision to divorce Mary is assumed to stem from an attitude of betrayal or from feeling upset with Mary. In most commentaries, it has been assumed that Joseph was expected to put Mary on trial to be executed for adultery.

The problem is that there is no direct mention of what Joseph was thinking. If we are going to read adultery, or scandal, or potential execution into the story it would pay to check whether such things are compatible with what is explicitly mentioned in the text.

In this book, text-based answers will be presented to these and other questions by attending to patterns in Matthew 1. I have tried to keep the presentation as logical as possible so as to be easy to follow not only for those who are Matthean scholars but for anyone interested in the study of Matthew.

The present book is laid out in ten chapters with summaries included at the beginning of each chapter. Any readers wanting a more exciting reading experience might prefer to skip the chapter overviews as these contain "spoilers." The book is structured in the following way.

Chapter 1 ("A Methodology for Answering Text-Based Questions") introduces the method for answering text-based questions with text-based observations, by attending to patterns such as repetitions, omissions, and symmetrical structures. These patterns contribute to the text's meaning and can be prioritized over other observations not drawn from the text.

Chapter 2 ("Framing the Messianic Lineage in Matt 1:1, 17") looks at how the Messiah comes to be the final heir according to verses 1 and 17. These two verses provide a framework for understanding the so-called genealogy (vv. 2–16). This framing identifies the Messiah as the culmination of his messianic lineage being a providential chosenness and inheritance from Abraham and David which culminates in the arrival of the final heir, the Messiah himself, whose lineage emerges from exile. It is necessary to be able to read this patriarchal-sounding lineage according to how it is framed if we want to understand how it might connect with how Joseph acquired Jesus as his heir according to verses 18–25, namely how verses 2–16 can be said to be Jesus's (non-biological) lineage.

Chapter 3 ("The Messianic Lineage in Matt 1:2–16") identifies the variations within the main formula of heir productions. Grammatically, the five references to mothers do not call attention to what the mothers did but call even further attention to what the fathers are said to have done (or not done in Joseph's case according to verse 16). In other words, it highlights the fathers' acquisition of their heirs (passively in Joseph's case, anticipating the story about to be explained in verses 18–25).

Chapter 4 ("Looking For Things Not There in Matt 1:18–25)" examines five popular reading assumptions that readers and hearers make which are not very compatible with the text, namely (1) conception; (2) scandal; (3) forbidden premarital sex; (4) expected execution; and (5) Joseph wrongly assuming adultery. Such assumptions have tended to drive the interpretation of verses 18–25 even though the focus, according to the story, is on *Joseph* rather than on Mary. Most of what popularly passes as "the story" turns out *not* to be in the text. It is necessary to become aware of what is not in the text if we want to understand the story according to the text rather than according to our own impositions and speculations.

Chapter 5 ("How Joseph is Right: The Poetics of Joseph's Necessary Plan in Matt 1:19") narrows down the focus to the topic of Joseph's providentially acquired paternity by examining how it was necessary for the story to inform us of Joseph's seemingly unnecessary plan, namely his double avoidance plan—planning not to claim Mary publicly as his wife but also planning not to disclaim her publicly as not being his wife (and not announcing his nonpaternity). Joseph only takes Mary because he was told to do so by an angel. Despite his initial reticence to raise a child he knew was not his, Joseph's parental status emerges providentially. Joseph's initial intentions play a key role in the story. It is necessary to understand how Joseph's initial intentions operate according to Matthew 1 unless we are happy to rely on speculation by importing ideas external to the text.

Chapter 6 ("What Kind of 'Genesis' is it in Matt 1:18?") looks at how Joseph son of David acquired Jesus as his son and gave him a divinely sanctioned name (alluding to Jesus's divinely sanctioned status and mission). Joseph acquires Jesus in his lineage which is identified as "how the Messiah Jesus's progeneration was" (τοῦ δὲ Ἰησοῦ χριστοῦ ἡ γένεσις οὕτως ἦν, verse 18a). Observing how the first five components in verses 18–25 pair up with the final five components reveals a concentric structure. The structure is necessary to observe if we want to understand what kind of "genesis" the second heading is referring to in verse 18a.

Chapter 7 ("The Poetics of Fulfillment in Matt 1:22") examines the central component in the second unit ("this whole thing took place so that what was spoken by the Lord through the prophet would be filled up") noting how the whole unit is permeated by the theme of culmination/

completion in order to explicate Joseph's unusual acquisition of his heir. This is necessary to observe if we want to understand what "this whole thing" refers to and why it "has happened" seemingly before much has actually happened.

Chapter 8 ("How Matt 1:18–25 Completes Matt 1:1–17") looks at how what is being completed in the second unit has been set up in the first unit. The acquisition of Joseph's heir connects back to the four earlier cases of how particular heirs were previously acquired. This is necessary to know because it means how Joseph passively acquired his heir is to be read in light of the four previously highlighted cases.

Chapter 9 ("The Parallel Scene to Matt 1:18–25 in Gen 38:24–26") examines the correspondences between Joseph's intentions in Matt 1:18–25 and Judah's intentions in the story of how he inadvertently produced Perez and Zerah from Tamar. The parallels reveal a similar genre at work in how Joseph's unplanned heir was anticipated in the story of Judah's discovery of Tamar's pregnancy. Joseph's initial response to Mary is meant to be contrasted with Judah's response to Tamar.

Chapter 10 ("The Pattern of the Five References to Mothers") examines the overall pattern of the five references to how the highlighted heirs were acquired in the Messiah's lineage, noting the correspondences in the topic of paternity between all five cases including the striking parallels between Boaz's acquisition of an heir (it is only in the genealogy in Ruth 4:18–22 that Obed is said to be Boaz's heir) and Joseph's acquisition of Jesus as his heir. The overall pattern is revealed to be a patriarchal pattern related to the making of, or determining of, an heir in each case.

In the epilogue, I briefly suggest how the same themes detected in Matthew 1 continue throughout Matthew. The overt patriarchal emphasis in Matthew would appear to be an important aspect within the rest of the book, not just Matthew 1.

There are five reasons why I have chosen to use the term "poetics" (from the Greek word ποιητικός "operative," "operation," "productive," or "production"). First, poetics identifies how something "works" or its "workings" (or its "makings"). To speak of the "poetics" of Matthew 1 is to speak of how Matthew 1 works as a system.

Second, poetics also refers to the individual literary techniques and linguistic patterns used by writers to compose a piece of literature. When we study the deliberate pattern of three groups of fourteen generations in the genealogical structure, or the repeated addition of the phrase "from a mother" ("from Tamar," "from Rahab," "from Ruth," "from her of Uriah," "from Mary"), or the concentric structure in verses 18–25, we are studying the poetics of Matthew 1. At times, "patterns" and "structures" are used interchangeable with the word "poetics."

Third, the topic of Matthew 1 concerns the Messiah's arrival, or how the Messiah "came to be" since Matthew 1 presents and explicates the ancestral lineage that "produced" the Messiah. So it is appropriate to speak of the poetics of the messianic "production."

Fourth, the term poetics was commonly used within literary studies in the 1980s for the study of biblical narrative literature as a term dating back to Aristotle's treatise on literary theory. Although the present book is not directly dependent on a particular literary theory or particular literary practice, the title is a nod to previous usage as a way to refer to the shaping of narrative-derived observations into a cohesive interpretation.

Finally, the term poetics also concerns how the text affects or "works on" its readers and hearers. The chapter that opens the New Testament demands to be read on its own terms as well as to be read ethically (the two are not mutually exclusive). The patriarchal nature of Matthew 1 stands out. The reading of a religious composition on a patriarchal topic makes the ethical issues identified in the text issues for its readers and hearers. Textual patterns are designed to be noticed and to exert influence on readers and hearers.

I

Methodology

Overview

This chapter outlines the method applicable to finding answers in the text for questions that are text based. Questions such as: *What is verse 22 referring to when it says, "All this has happened" (seemingly before it has all happened)?* and, *Why are there five references to mothers in the Messiah's genealogy?* are text-based questions which might lead us to seek and find text-based answers. Such a method is not entirely new but it is usually supplemented and supplanted by other methods which rely heavily on details external to the text. It is essential to notice what we usually import into the text (things not there) and to notice what seem like redundancies in the text (things that seem unnecessary). It is also important to notice what seems contradictory to what we think the text is trying to say. Interpretive ideas that we think are helping the text to make sense can distract us from seeing what is in the text.

Asking text-based questions

THE PRESENT METHOD IS most similar to that practiced by Rabbi David Fohrman in the study of the Jewish Tanakh (what Christians call the Old Testament), particularly as Fohrman applies it to the book of Genesis.[1]

In short, the method involves identifying basic literary questions that arise from reading (questions that seem necessary to ask of the text) and then answering these question using observable literary patterns within the text for clues to meaning.

Questions concerning *who* or *what* are generally easier to answer than questions about *how* or *why* something is or is not mentioned. For example,

---

1. Fohrman, *Genesis: A Parsha Companion.*

the questions, *Who gives Joseph a message?* and, *What message is given to Joseph in Matthew 1?* can be easily answered according to the story. *How* the messenger is presented, or *how* the angel communicates to Joseph is also relatively easy to identify, namely the angel appears to Joseph in a dream and gives Joseph an instruction and a birth prophecy. But the question, *Why in a dream?* is more complex to answer as it involves a much deeper understanding of the combination of interactions being narrated and may or may not be answerable even after much in-depth study.

Some questions are obviously not the right kind of question that can be answered literarily (according to the text). For example, *Who else is already living in the same house as Joseph?* is a question for which the text offers no answer. Similarly, *How much did Jesus weigh at birth?* is not something that Matthew 1 answers or was meant to answer.

There are, however, certain text-based questions that arise for commentators attempting to make sense of Matthew 1 that seem necessary for the text to answer and yet the answers have remained undiscovered in the text.

For example, before Mary has been accepted by Joseph and before she has given birth verse 22 says, "this has all happened" yet seemingly before it has all happened. We might imagine that verse 22 would work better as a conclusion to the story vignette after the story has taken place. Why does it say "this has happened" if it really means to say that all this *will soon have happened*? Answering this question is necessary unless we resign ourselves to not being able to know what verse 22 refers to.

This question was often asked throughout the middle ages. For example, according to Thomas Aquinas's collection of ancient commentary on Matthew, the ninth-century Benedictine monk Remigius commented:

> Here we must enquire why he [Matthew] should say "all this was done," when above he has only related the conception. It should be known that he says this to shew, that in the presence of God "all this was done" before it was done among men.[2]

Remigius then offers a more compositional answer, "Or he [Matthew] says, 'all' this was done, because he is relating past events; for when he wrote, it was all done." To say that it had already happened would make sense if verse 22 is giving the perspective of the person writing the account, looking back from the future.

---

2. Remigius on Matt 1:18 in Aquinas, *Catena Aurea*.

John Chrysostom combined a theological and narrative solution when he said that the expression ("all this has happened") indicated what the angel had now witnessed and what had just been undertaken theologically, namely a miraculous conception and "reconciliation made."[3]

A more text-based answer can be seen in Anselm's solution. Anselm noticed four things that were mentioned prior to verse 22, namely that "the Virgin was betrothed" (v. 18); "she was kept chase" (vv. 18–19); "she was found with child" (v. 18); and "the revelation was made by the Angel" (v. 20).[4] Anselm has tried to identify things that have already occurred in the text in order to explain what verse 22 is referring to when it says, "All this has been done." This kind of solution is closer to the present methodology because Anselm has attempted to find text-based answers for text-based questions.

Some questions have previously been misidentified as *questions not answered in the text*. Note the following text-based questions and how we usually answer them.

Why is Jesus not biologically related to his genealogy? The question is usually answered by imagining that the first seventeen verses of human ancestry are somewhat unnecessary as though Matt 1:1–17 and 1:18–25 might reflect two different sources.

What does verse 22 refer to when it says "all this has happened?" The question is often answered by thinking of it as an intrusion from a future perspective into the story's chronology, or that it really belongs with the conclusion.

Exactly what kind of "genesis" is meant when it refers to the Messiah's "progeneration" (γένεσις) in verse 18? The question is usually answered by guessing birth, conception, or general circumstances leading up to birth.

Why does verse 17 highlight a structural pattern of three groups of fourteen generations in the Messiah's genealogy? The question is usually answered by supposing it is numerological, indicating the number of David.

Why are there five references to mothers in the Messiah's genealogy? The question is usually answered by guessing that it has something to do with the women's race, ethnicity, gender, status, or alleged sexual scandals.

The usual answers to the above questions depend on making educated guesses by relying on ideas from *outside* the text. Yet the above questions are not questions arising out of historical curiosity—they are text-based (literary)

---

3. Chrysostom on Matt 1:18 in Aquinas, *Catena Aurea*.

4. Anselm on Matt 1:18 in Aquinas, *Catena Aurea*.

questions arising from an attempt to understand the text on its own terms. We should expect the text to have answers for such questions.

The text is more informative than we tend to allow

Those of us who are commentators of Matthew have a tendency to underestimate how informative the text might be when we are tempted to look for answers elsewhere. Looking beyond the text for historical context makes sense when asking historically-based questions. But for text-based questions it is more logical that we look for text-based answers. By observing similarities between one verse and another in Matthew 1 we can increase our understanding of not only how each verse operates but also our understanding of the combined function of such verses.

For example, studying verse 17 can facilitate noticeable similarities with verse 1. These similarities can assist in the understanding of both verses which then can assist in understanding the lineage as framed by these verses. What might be so significant about specifying "fourteen generations" for each group ("from Abraham until David," "from David until the Babylonian exile," and "from the Babylonian exile until the Messiah") does not need to depend on speculation. Also, some of us refuse to accept what verse 17 says about the third group, namely that there are fourteen generations from the time of the Babylonian exile until the Messiah (if we choose not to count Jechoniah in the third group).[5]

In the commentaries, "fourteen" is usually guessed to be a triple reference to the "number" of David (since the letters in David's name in Hebrew would add up, numerically, to "fourteen"). But why *three* cryptic references, in Greek, to David's Hebrew number? Pointing out a *single* group of fourteen would have achieved the same goal. And why is the end point of the second group not an ancestor but an event? If David is fourteenth because his "number" is fourteen, why is exile also numbered as "fourteen"? It seems the point of verse 17 was to explain the *entire* ancestral lineage in three stages by noting how *each* group culminates.

Verse 17 is, or should be, commentators' gold since the text offers a commentary on the whole genealogical account given in verses 2–16. It highlights a structural pattern and mentions a purpose with "therefore" (οὖν) and mentions the overall timing with "until [the time of]" (ἕως). Verse 17 draws attention to a progressive pattern indicating that something

5. For a method which includes Jechoniah, see Carlson, "The Davidic Key," 665–83.

significant culminates with the fourteenth generation three times (David; exile; Messiah) as though outlining the Messiah's arrival within the context of the entire three-stage ancestry.

By summarizing everything in verses 2–16, verse 17 invites us to notice the "timing" as though things are operating within a cosmic kind of calendar. The timing in this cosmic calendar is beyond ordinary human operation (and not even noticed by humans until afterwards). In other words, the Messiah arrived in a providentially timed way as the identifiable pattern is not merely coincidental. Apparently, the Messiah's arrival was always on the divine agenda, at least since Abraham. The operative pattern presents a providentially shaped lineage which is similar to how the heading functions in verse 1 (which identifies a sacred story of a providentially given lineage for the Messiah's arrival).

Sometimes, as in this case, the answer in the text is not radically new or surprising since commentators already suspected that a providential theme is playing out in Matthew 1.

How the Messiah arrives in Matthew 1 is based on several patterns, including the pattern of timing (the three "fourteens"); the pattern of a narrated genealogy (not just listed names but the use of a father-produced-son formula); the five additional references to sons produced "from a mother"; an interdependent pattern of human-divine coordination; a concentric pattern (vv. 18–25) with a fulfillment formula at the center; along with other "patterns" of things intentionally "missing" or avoided.

The pertinent literary (text-based) questions raised above will be answered by observing and examining such patterns.

Identifying things not in the text

Identifying what is and what is not in the text is complex. Some things we might assume to be missing might not be missing and some things we assume to be present might not be present.

Having no mention of a conversation taking place between Mary and Joseph before Joseph makes a decision in verse 19 is usually identified as a "gap" in the story. Also, the text seems not to have mentioned what Joseph was thinking when he decided he would quietly divorce Mary. If the reasoning for Joseph's plan is missing and the conversation with Mary is missing it might seem logical for an audience to have to find answers beyond the text in order to fill these "gaps" in the story.

Our earliest surviving commentaries on Matthew fill these alleged gaps by offering three interpretations of Joseph's reticence. Either (a) Joseph was afraid of being married to a presumably adulterous woman; or (b) he feared a miraculous pregnancy and never doubted Mary's innocence; or (c) Joseph was indecisive, hovering between (a) and (b).

The most fascinating example of an "unsure Joseph" hovering between (a) and (b) is found in an ancient Syriac dialogue poem in which Mary and Joseph take turns eloquently debating their perspectives concerning Mary's conception and pregnancy.[6] Mary almost manages to fully convince Joseph that her pregnancy is a miraculously conceived pregnancy, thereby almost shifting Joseph from thinking (a) to thinking (b). By imagining Mary into the scene, the Syriac dialogue poem deals with these two alleged "gaps" in the story by expanding on Matt 1:19 in which Joseph is deciding on the matter and discussing it with Mary.[7]

However, an analysis of Joseph's response will reveal that we are not expected to assume that Mary tries unsuccessfully to explain the situation to Joseph. To do so is to miss the intended point of the story. There is plenty within the story to account for Joseph's behavior, including the basis for Joseph's decision.

The attempt to identify things "missing" is, at least, a helpful starting point since part of the process of observing how the text works is to become conscious of when we are importing things into the text.

The issue is more complex than usually supposed. Consider the late tenth-century paraphrase of Matt 1:18–25 that appears at the end of the *Nativity of Mary* in which the writer has relayed apocryphal stories of things not included in the Gospel according to Matthew (giving various childhood stories of Mary and childhood stories of Jesus). Having given sufficient apocryphal stories predating and postdating Jesus's birth, the writer then returns to the birth of Jesus according to "the Gospel" by paraphrasing Matt 1:18–25 within the framework of Luke's geographical journey to (and from) Bethlehem. The 10th-century Latin paraphrase is of Matt 1:18–25 but I quote here only what corresponds to verse 18b:

6. Brock, *Treasure-House of Mysteries*, 144–51.

7. For a modern example of this sort of approach, see Branch, "When Mary Tells Joseph."

Greek-English Diglot (Matt 1:18b)		Tenth-century Paraphrase
πρὶν ἢ συνελθεῖν αὐτοὺς εὑρέθη ἐν γαστρὶ ἔχουσα ἐκ πνεύματος ἁγίου. (SBLGNT)	Before they came together she was already having in belly from the Holy Spirit	Meanwhile, the womb of the woman to give birth gradually grew as the child to be born began to show. Nor could it be concealed from Joseph. As is customary for betrothed men, he freely entered into the Virgin's home and spoke with her, and realized that she was pregnant.[8]

From a modern vantage point, it might seem that the above paraphrase is filling in the story with apocryphal details, as if it adds the "missing" detail of how Joseph found out Mary was pregnant.

But the idea that Joseph discovers Mary's pregnancy by seeing her enlarged belly might not be something lacking from the story. The manner in which verse 18b mentions Mary being discernibly pregnant is concise and ambiguous. "Her having a pregnant belly from the Holy Spirit" is something that "became known" or "was found (to be)." To whom Mary's belly was discernibly a pregnant belly is ambiguous but not necessarily missing. Not only is the story's audience informed of the pregnancy, Joseph may also be aware of it, especially given that the following sentence (v. 19) presents Joseph's response to it. So, in verse 18b, Joseph himself might be included in the verb such that Mary's belly "became evident" to Joseph.

The idea that Joseph noticed Mary's belly is actually based on the ambiguity present in the text that potentially includes Joseph in the verb, as though *Joseph saw that Mary was pregnant*. Modern commentators often take the ambiguity in verse 18b as an indication that the text has neglected to mention how Joseph found out that Mary was pregnant and we might think that the paraphrase at the end of the *Nativity of Mary* is importing an idea from outside the text. But more likely, the paraphrase takes it that verse 18b indicates that Joseph realizes *when he saw* Mary's belly (while talking with her one day). The idea of having a visit and a chat with Mary is a more extreme extrapolation of the same idea of Joseph *seeing* Mary.

After Joseph sees that Mary is pregnant there is a conspicuous absence of interaction with Mary within the story. There is nothing in the text to indicate that Joseph consulted Mary about her pregnancy. If we cannot

---

8. Hawk, *Gospel of Pseudo-Matthew*, 140.

account for this absence by appealing to the text, it would be wise to refrain from importing a "missing" discussion of the pregnancy if we claim to be interpreting the text as we have it rather than looking for, and interpreting, an alternate version of the story.

The task of identifying which interpretations are unnecessary importations is difficult when they have already become entrenched in our interpretations. In some cases we have become so familiar with what we assume the text is saying that it is almost impossible to distinguish between our own assumptions and the text.

For example, the kind of vocabulary used in the speech given to Joseph by an angel in verse 20 does not conform to what we assume is there since the unborn Jesus is referred to as "the born one" (τὸ γεννηθὲν). It usually goes unnoticed that the language of "conceived" is missing:

> τὸ γὰρ ἐν αὐτῇ γεννηθὲν ἐκ πνεύματός ἐστιν ἁγίου.
>
> (For) the (one) born in her is from the Holy Spirit.

Ancient readers, like Basil of Caesarea, noticed it:

> Οὐ γὰρ εἴρηται, Τὸ κυνηθὲν, ἀλλὰ, «Τὸ γεννηθέν»
>
> For it does not say, "The conceived," but, "The born."[9]

Basil concluded that Jesus must have arrived in Mary's womb fully formed. Augustine thought the significance of Christ's being twice born ("in her" as well as "from her") parallels a double birth of Christians.[10]

One way that ancient readers dealt with the issue was to add what was assumed to be missing when translating "the one born," namely by translating it as "the one born in her *is conceived*" (as in the Curetonian Syriac translation).[11] Other Syriac translations declined to "fix" the problem. Therefore, Ishodad of Merv (ninth century) felt it necessary to comment on the use of "the born one" in Syriac:

> It is asked, why does Matthew say "the one born in her is from the Holy Spirit" when He [Jesus] was not yet born and he [Matthew] did not say the one conceived in her? Also [saying], the one "born in her" and not "born from her?"[12]

---

9. Basil of Caesarea, "On the Holy Nativity," PG 31, 1465.

10. Boulding, *Expositions of the Psalms*, 127.

11. For the Syriac see Kiraz, *Comparative Edition*, 11.

12. For the Syriac, see Gibson, *The Commentaries of Isho'dad*, 21.

Ishodad noted several different solutions, rejecting the allegation that the expression "born in her" might originally have been "conceived in her."

At some point along the way, commentators stopped noticing the difference here because they assumed that τὸ γεννηθὲν must be indicating conception. What else would the writer of the text be trying to say? Inevitably, it is tempting for commentators to simply paraphrase τὸ ἐν αὐτῇ γεννηθὲν as though it refers to Mary's pregnancy that she has conceived ("that which has been conceived in her") failing to observe that the text as we read it is not the text as we have it. It would be more fruitful for us to observe the omission of conception or to consider why the prophecy is already speaking of Mary's child by using the language of "born" at this point.

Explaining other omissions in the text is also important. Can we explain why Sarah and Rebecca are omitted from the Messiah's lineage? It could have said, "Abraham produced Isaac from Sarah; Isaac produced Jacob from Rebecca." Verse 3 has not included the mothers of Jacob's children even though it might have included them by saying, "Jacob produced Judah and his brothers from Leah, Rachel, Zilpah and Bilhah." Why omit the first few mothers when other mothers are not omitted?

We might be tempted to look for a pattern with the mothers who *are* included without attempting to explain the mothers who are *not* included. For example, if we suppose that the final heir production is a story about Mary's miraculous pregnancy we would also need to explain why Sarah is omitted since Sarah also had a miraculous pregnancy.[13]

Also, Sarah was involved in an apparent sex scandal just prior to her pregnancy when she was taken as a wife or concubine by King Abimelech (Gen 20:1–18) after she and Abraham had told people they were brother and sister (implying Sarah was unmarried). If we suppose that the five included mothers reflect stories of sex scandals, we need to explain why Sarah was not included.

If we suppose that Ruth is included because she is a non-Judean coming from a place outside of Judea then again we must ask why not include the Aramaean/Chaldean matriarch Sarah who, likewise, is a non-Judean born in a foreign land? Ruth is not much more foreign than Sarah according to the book of Ruth since Ruth ultimately comes from the same lineage as Abraham's father Terah (like Sarah!). Matthew 1 does not reference Ruth's

---

13. Miller notes, "If Matthew had wanted to prepare readers for a miraculous birth, he could have mentioned Sarah, mother of Isaac, and Rachel mother of Joseph—both of whom reportedly conceived through miracles—instead of Tamar, Rahab, Ruth, and Bathsheba." Miller, "The Illegitimacy of Jesus," 35.

ethnicity or the ethnicity of any of the mentioned mothers which would have been easy to mention if that were the point in Matthew 1.

We might want to check whether the pattern we choose to read into the text is fully compatible with the text. If we are going to propose a pattern with the mothers who are *included* without adequately explaining the *excluded* mothers we have not adequately explained the text. If Sarah would also fit our theorized pattern, we might need to admit that our hypothetical pattern does not adequately fit the text as we have it.

What about the lack of time references mentioning when Mary was initially betrothed to Joseph or how long until the wedding or how many months Mary had already been pregnant or how many months later it was that she gave birth? Interpreters often import such details into the story in order to help the story along. But such additions can end up becoming the framework for interpreting the story. This is not the text-driven framework required to observe the poetics of the text.

Becoming aware of what is not in the text can take time. A classic example in the history of interpretation of Matthew 1 is that verse 25 ("he did not have intimate relations with her up till the time she gave birth to a son") was often thought to imply something about whether Mary and Joseph remained a celibate couple *after* Jesus was born, namely whether they then commenced a regular sexual relationship. It was common to interpret the verse along such lines despite Jerome's observation that, "Scripture however shews not what did happen."[14] Nowadays it is more widely recognized that the postnatal status of Mary and Joseph's sexual relationship is not in the text. It is only there for those who assume it is. It is no mere coincidence that those who already think that the text speaks of a commencement of postnatal sex are those who suppose that Mary and Joseph went on to produce other children whilst those who think that the reason the text mentions the celibacy again in verse 25 (it was previously mentioned in verse 18) are those who see that this highlights the celibacy within the holy marriage undertaken as ordained by the divine plan. Both readings had their sights set too far afield by not being restricted by the text but instead expecting the text to answer wider historical questions. Both interpretations overestimated what is in verses 18–25.

We might become aware of things not in the text in four ways. An obvious one is when the text asserts that something is not meant to be read in. For example, the desire to shame Mary is said to be lacking from Joseph's

14. Jerome on Matt 1:18 in Aquinas, *Catena Aurea*.

intention in verse 19. When it says Joseph did not want to shame her, it provides a negative assertion stating that something is absent. If we were to think that Joseph *did* intend to do or say something to shame Mary then we would not be reading with the text but against the text.

Another way to notice when something is not meant to be there is when a positive assertion in the text prevents a negative implication. A positive statement can deflect against potential negative connotations that otherwise might have arisen had the positive statement not been there. For example, by saying "her having a pregnant belly *from the Holy Spirit* became apparent" (rather than simply saying "her having a pregnant belly became apparent") it discourages readers and hearers from inferring something negative about Mary's pregnancy. Those of us who might infer something negative about Mary's pregnancy should know that such an inference is coming from outside the text not within it.

Thirdly, we might notice that something is simply not there. Some things are simply not there because they were never intended to be there, in which case we are not expected to read them in. For example, the postnatal sex life of Mary and Joseph is not present in Matthew 1.

Fourthly, the most difficult and intriguing kind of absence to study is when something is not there but we are expected to read it in. For example, we are told that Joseph initially decided he would divorce Mary rather than accept Mary as his wife. But adultery is not mentioned. Most interpreters conclude that the reason for Joseph's decision is that Joseph must have been thinking about how Mary has conceived (by adultery) and thus judging her to have been an unfaithful wife. This might explain why he could not accept her. In this case, we would be reading something into the text. Adultery is never mentioned in the text. Yet perhaps we are supposed to read something like adultery into what Joseph was thinking. So we would need to become conscious of the reasons for reading it in and to consider whether there are other interpretations that might make better sense of the text.

It would be helpful if we could let go of the idea that "exegesis" (reading out of the text) is the opposite of "eisegesis" (reading into the text) since we are expected to read some things into the text. It seems we are expected to be able to understand Joseph's motivation for divorce even though the text does not expressly mention what Joseph was thinking. Consciously reading something into the text is a necessary part of the exegetical process. The kind of conscious eisegesis in feminist interpretation ultimately leads to a better exegetical understanding of how the text works since it encourages us to identify what we want the text to be saying and to become aware of how that might be affecting our interpretation.

Identifying redundancies

We can also identify what seems like it is not required even though included. When something in the text seems unessential it is likely a sign of misunderstanding on our part.

One example is the verb "produced" that appears throughout the genealogy for every heir produced (ἐγέννησεν thirty-nine times; ἐγεννήθη once). It may be tempting to think of the verb as not always necessary (some English versions will skip over the repetition or use a different verb for its final appearance in the passive form in verse 16).

Similarly, verse 17 might not seem to be adding much new to what has already been narrated in verses 2–16 since the three groups were already marked within the genealogy itself (the first group of fourteen generations ended with the addition of the epithet "the king" in verse 6; the second group of generations ended with the addition of the expression "at the time of the Babylonian deportation" in verse 11; and the third group ended with the epithet "the one called Messiah" in verse 16). So the three-part structure was already marked with three additional annotations for the three endpoints. We might wonder what verse 17 adds to the text.

Also, the second textual unit (vv. 18–25) begins by narrating that Joseph initially decided not to pursue marriage with Mary as though this is important information for us to know at this point. What might the text be trying to achieve by narrating Joseph's plan to divorce Mary? Did we really need to know about Joseph's almost rejection of Mary?

Also, there are several seemingly redundant mentions of Mary and Joseph's marital status. Verse 16 mentions their marital status as husband and wife; so does verse 18; so does verse 19; so does verse 20; and so does verse 24. For such a succinctly told story vignette, this many mentions might not seem necessary.

Identifying seemingly contradictory elements

Another important principle for observing how the text works is to identify what seem like contradictions within the text. For example, why is it that the story introduces Joseph as someone who is right-acting ("righteous") if an angel has to intervene in order to stop Joseph from doing what we assume is not the right thing (because apparently Joseph cannot be bothered listening to Mary and is motivated by wrong assumptions about how she became pregnant)? Is the man who thought that Mary was a cheat and/or a liar really being held up as "righteous"? The story seems to be contradictory. It would appear that our previous explanations are not successfully answering the pertinent questions arising from the text because they have not been adequately derived from the text.

Chiastic structures are there to help

The concentric structure of Matt 1:18–25 is not there simply for fun or beauty. The chiastic structure holds the unit together functionally as well as aesthetically. When every component has a matching component (on the "opposite" side of the center of the unit), each component is informed by its counterpart so that we can read one in light of the other. If we find one component too ambiguous, the matching component can assist us.

Being familiar with the structure also provides the interpreter with a tool to assess other interpretations. For example, if someone were to suggest that the final clause "he called his name Jesus" belongs not to Matthew 1 but belongs to the beginning of Matthew 2, we might not have any good reason to judge such an interpretation without knowing that the concentric structure requires it to belong to Matthew 1. Similarly, if we encounter an interpretation conjecturing that the penultimate clause did not originally include the phrase ἕως οὗ ("until such time when") we would not otherwise have any text-based reason to query such a conjecture.[15]

In sum, the method is not particularly new but, by looking to the text for answers, it asks that the interpretative focus be much more limited than what is usually undertaken by expecting that the text might answer its own literary questions. Basically it involves identifying things that are and are not in the text and observing linguistic and thematic patterns for clues to

---

15. Schatkin examines why the text puts the birth of Jesus "in a subordinate clause (ἕως οὗ) [to Joseph's sexual continence] and disconnects the birth syntactically from the naming" which leads her to conjecture that the clause originally ended after καὶ οὐκ ἐγίνωσκεν αὐτὴν such that "ὁμοῦ τε ἔτεκεν υἱόν" becomes the next clause. Schatkin, "The Perpetual Virginity of Mary," 62. Yet the chiastic structure speaks against a textual emendation here since the text as we have it matches the second sentence of the unit where a similar time clause also subordinates the pregnancy to a comment on the lack of sexual union (πρὶν ἢ συνελθεῖν αὐτούς).

meaning. It asks that interpreters notice what seems missing, redundant, or contradictory as these things are critical to distinguishing between our own impositions and text-driven interpretations.

2

Framing the Messianic Lineage in Matt 1:1, 17

Overview

This chapter examines verses 1 and 17 as the framing for verses 2–16. The opening verse is an introductory heading for the Messiah's "genesis" or "coming to be" which can be translated, provisionally, as "lineage." Verse 17 is a concluding summary for the lineage. We can understand the lineage according to how it is framed. Both verse 1 and verse 17 are densely packed. Verse 1 introduces a providential plan. Verse 17 reveals that the one called Messiah arrived in a providentially timed way. As well as identifying the heritage of the Messiah, it identifies a sacred storyline revealing the kind of Messiah who arrives with a mission and implies an ongoing legacy. Jesus is identified as "chosen" (anointed). Like David, and like Abraham, the Messiah is divinely appointed. According to verse 17 he is also heir to an "exilic" paradigm. The Messiah does not arrive to replicate Davidic kingship but to rectify it.

Greek-English Diglot (Matt 1:1)

Βίβλος γενέσεως Ἰησοῦ Χριστοῦ υἱοῦ Δαυὶδ υἱοῦ Ἀβραάμ (SBLGNT)	Book of Genesis of Jesus Messiah Son of David Son of Abraham

THE FIRST VERSE IS not a complete sentence but a densely compact heading containing no verbs or definite articles. It is composed of a noun (βίβλος) followed by seven nouns in the genitive case. Each noun is grammatically dependent on the following noun to narrow the meaning, thereby producing a string of eight nouns.

The first word (βίβλος) informs of an unfolding "plan" or "schema" of a "divine intention" or "sacred story." Thus *biblos* (βίβλος) is a numinous kind of "blueprint" outlining something supernatural, particularly used for speaking of divinely inspired content, or a "sacred book."[1] When hearing verse 1 read aloud, there is a slight pause for breath after the eighth word, Ἀβραάμ, audibly connecting the first and eighth words. In a single breath we hear of a providential plan (βίβλος) that is somehow related to Abraham. The eight nouns pair up neatly into four pairs:

1st pair	2nd pair	3rd pair	4th pair
βίβλος γενέσεως	Ἰησοῦ χριστοῦ	υἱοῦ Δαυὶδ	υἱοῦ Ἀβραάμ
Book of Genesis	(of) Jesus Messiah	(of) Son of David	(of) Son of Abraham

The middle two pairs function almost synonymously ("Jesus Messiah"; "son of David") and the two outer pairs also suggest similarities in which "book of Genesis" pairs with "son of Abraham" just as the original "book of Genesis" concerned Abraham obtaining an heir, tracing the legacy or chosen "seed" of Abraham. In this way, the book of Matthew immediately associates itself with the Abraham story from the original book of Genesis, as though to present one more biblical story or lineage to continue the earlier stories and lineages begun in Genesis.

At this stage, prior to verse 2, we might not think of the kind of intended "schema" as outlining Jesus's ancestry. It is not necessary to read the terms "son of David" and "son of Abraham" as genealogical labels (a more genealogical label would have been "Jesus son of Joseph, son of Jacob"). The terms "son of David" and "son of Abraham" are more like titles indicative of the kind of role that Jesus will have as the next one "chosen" (χριστός) by God for a particular mission.

The content of the providential plan (βίβλος) concerns Jesus (Ἰησοῦ) as Messiah (χριστοῦ) identified as the "anointed one" or "chosen leader" presenting Jesus's messianic status and mission.

The tendency in English Bibles to take the heading as a genealogical heading underestimates the importance of the very first word, *biblos* (βίβλος, literally "papyrus" but it refers to the content, not the fabric, of the document). Unlike the content of a *biblion* (βιβλίον being any kind of

---

1. See Mark 12:26; Luke 3:4; 20:42; Acts 1:20; 7:42; 19:19; Phil 4:3; Rev 3:5; 20:15.

document) the content of a *biblos* reveals a divine intention. In this case, the divine plan to bring the Messiah.

The same heading already appeared in Gen 5:1 for introducing the original lineage and storyline of humans in the "book of progeneration of humankind" (LXX: βίβλος γενέσεως ἀνθρώπων; Hebrew: סֵפֶר תּוֹלְדֹת אָדָם). The following lineage (vv. 2–16) can be read in light of this very "biblical" sounding heading.

The second word, γενέσεως, is "existence." The kind of existence, in this case, is the Messiah's coming-to-be. The Messiah's arrival is providentially determined to be. The modern tendency is to jump quickly from a more general idea ("life"; "existence") to a more specific idea ("ancestral lineage") as though the meaning must be narrowed down to a single sense in order for us to proceed. However, the earliest audiences were probably not thinking like modern lexicographers and would not assume that the Messiah's coming-to-be must be limited in a narrow sense to mean only heritage.

In fact, even if audiences are already thinking of the following ancestral lineage, they would probably still notice that this is not merely presenting a heritage but also presupposes a *legacy* for the Messiah. To offer a biblical-sounding written account concerning the Messiah is enough of a clue that the story is considered to have ongoing relevance for its readers and hearers. The heading is not simply introducing some trivial details out of historical curiosity. Rather, it seems that this Jesus Messiah has come to usher in a new era. He, like Abraham, has a legacy in which his coming is significant for a people who now look to him as their eponymous leader. So the Messiah's coming is dependent on a heritage but also suggestive of an ongoing legacy with ongoing status.

Every word of verse 1 is indispensable in the sense that if a single one of these eight words were omitted, the meaning would be significantly affected. The final two pairs of words ("heir of David" and "heir of Abraham") highlight the foregoing words as being defined by these words and segue into the following Davidic-Abrahamic lineage (vv. 2–16). The string of genitive relationships specifies that the one who is the "heir of" is the one who is the "inheritor in the vein of David who himself inherited Abraham." The providentially chosen inheritance is the theme. In fact, the fourth, fifth, sixth, seventh, and eighth nouns all promote "chosenness," that is, the one anointed (by God), heir (of) David, heir (of) Abraham.

The kind of plan in view is a providential storyline of progeneration (βίβλος γενέσεως). Essentially, verse 1 is saying that the designation of the final/ultimate heir (the Messiah himself) is something chosen by God (as it was also, previously, in the case David and Abraham). The following lineage plots this appointed status as a storyline.

Verse 17 adds another layer of interpretation by reviewing this biblical storyline and explaining it in terms of a three-part paradigm. Like verse 1, it does this without using a single verb (reserving the verb for the lineage itself).

Greek-English Diglot (Matt 1:17)

Πᾶσαι οὖν αἱ γενεαὶ ἀπὸ Ἀβραὰμ ἕως Δαυὶδ γενεαὶ δεκατέσσαρες, καὶ ἀπὸ Δαυὶδ ἕως τῆς μετοικεσίας Βαβυλῶνος γενεαὶ δεκατέσσαρες, καὶ ἀπὸ τῆς μετοικεσίας Βαβυλῶνος ἕως τοῦ χριστοῦ γενεαὶ δεκατέσσαρες. (SBLGNT)	So all the generations from Abraham until David are fourteen generations, and from David until the Babylonian exile fourteen generations, and from the Babylonian exile until the Messiah fourteen generations.

It is no accident that verse 17 corresponds to the heading in verse 1. Matt 1:17 not only contains three of the same nouns (Abraham; David; Messiah) but these three nouns appear in reverse order to verse 1 (Messiah; David; Abraham), thereby highlighting a connection with verse 1, together framing the ancestral lineage.[2]

Like the first pair of nouns in verse 1 (βίβλος γενέσεως), verse 17 indicates divine providence when it highlights a pattern of three fourteens. Thus the lineage is framed as a providential story. The way each "fourteen" culminates is meant to show that the Messiah's arrival accords with a divine kind of plan which is neither random nor sudden. In verse 17, the ancestry is grouped into three parts with three summary headings ("from the time of Abraham until the time of David," and "from the time of David until the time of Babylonian exile" and "from the time of Babylonian exile until the Messiah"). The equal sized proportions indicate the cyclical nature of the "timing" or overall "timeline" for the Messiah's arrival presenting a three-part mythic paradigm of cosmic proportions, charting a grand plan reflecting the divine agenda to bring the leader for a new era (the Messiah himself) who arrives on time.

---

2. Weren notes, "The trio of 1:1 reappear in reversed order in 1:17: Abraham, David, the Messiah. This concluding verse has the same function as 1:1. Together they give structure to the genealogy." Weren, *Studies in Matthew's Gospel*, 110.

It is almost as if "fourteen" is indicative of "cycles of (re)production" or "fecundity," or a three-part process of "maturation" or as though "fourteen" itself signifies periods of "gestation." Considering the two other repeated words γενεαὶ ("generations") and ἐγέννησεν ("he progenerated") it invokes a "culmination" of production. Fourteen is working here within a domain of productive cycles or stages of culmination, as though to say, "Abraham culminates in David; David culminates in exile; exile culminates in the Messiah—note the symmetry!"

The timing within this cosmic calendar means that the rise and demise of Davidic kingship occurs on the same "date" (the "fourteenth"). Likewise the Messiah also arrives on the same "date" as the exile (loss of kingship, land, and Temple). The three groups in verse 17 present a cycle of birth, death, and resurrection, namely the birth of a Davidic kingship followed by its loss or "death" (in the Babylonian exile) then followed by the eventual emergence of the new leader, the one called Messiah.[3] The paradigmatic nature of the three part ancestry also anticipates the life, death, and resurrection of the story of Jesus's own life about to be narrated in the remainder of the book.

Notably, the life of the Messiah is divinely intended, being influenced by ancestry and being identified as having a divine purpose and being an influencer of things to come. Therefore the meaning of the Messiah's "genesis" in verse 1 is not to be narrowed down to one sense. Rather, it indicates:

a. The ancestry which produced Jesus the Messiah; and

b. The life as product; the life produced; the life story or life mission of Jesus as the Messiah; and

c. The legacy that the life of Jesus produced.

If our goal is to find a minimal reading for the Messiah's kind of "genesis" we would somehow need to eliminate both (a) and (c) as though we could extract Jesus's own distinctive life from the influences stretching back before and the influences continuing on from his life. In this case, the minimal interpretation for the Messiah's genesis would be "life" or "life mission" according to verse 1.

---

3. Scott comments similarly concerning the pattern of time in the book of Jubilees, "the proof of the existence of divine providence . . . is in its rhythmic working in history: construction, deconstruction, reconstruction. All this was decreed from heaven to occur in periods that were equal in length and therefore symmetrical." Scott, *On Earth as in Heaven*, 213.

But we might want to take into account the entire ancestry (vv. 2–16) as being what influenced or led up to the life of Jesus Messiah. Then we might eventually finish reading the entire book and notice the greater significance and effects that the life of Jesus has apparently "produced" (including post-death). Consequently, it is almost impossible to restrict the application for the Messiah's kind of genesis in verse 1 as simply "life produced" since Jesus's life is not independent of causes and effects. According to verse 1 and verse 17, it is seen as a product both "influenced by" and as "influencing of" other people and events.

So γένεσις ("life"), on one side is something "influenced by" ("heritage") and on the other side is an "influencer of" ("legacy") such that "distinctive life" is "derivative" of what "caused" it at one side and at the other side is seen to be "generative" of what it has "caused."

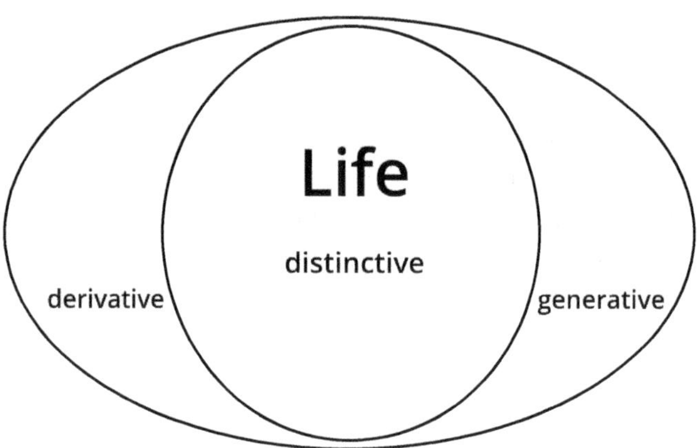

Figure 1. Spectrum of "life" (γένεσις).

We do not need to side only with either a "derivative" or a "generative" meaning. Being the chosen leader includes both.[4] The Messiah's kind of "genesis" includes not only "heritage" but "distinct life" and "legacy."

For heritage: note "heir of David, heir of Abraham" (v. 1) along with the given ancestry (vv. 2–16); note also "Joseph heir of David" (v. 20).

---

4. Classen makes a similar point, "for the evangelist seems to want his readers to understand both the factors leading up to and those resulting from the generation." Classen, *Rhetorical Criticism*, 76.

For life purpose or distinct life: note βίβλος (v. 1) which indicates a particular story as does verse 17 (a providentially guided account); γενέσεως (v. 1) suggests characteristic nature; χριστός (v. 1 and v. 16) suggests a life mission; verse 21 identifies the distinct life mission ("to save his people from their sins").

For legacy: note the continued status of Jesus the Messiah is assumed in Matt 1:1; note that identifying Jesus as Messiah (v. 16) expressly anticipates a time when he is "said to be 'Messiah'" by others; likewise verse 17 implies something paradigmatic as if anticipating a new era now begun since the Messiah's arrival; verse 23 suggests a continued legacy of being called "God with Us" by future generations; and the book ends with Jesus declaring "I will always be with you" (Matt 28:20 the "you" inclusive of future audiences).

In all, the title βίβλος γενέσεως is a fitting way to begin the book we call Matthew.[5] Understandably, the early church chose to begin the New Testament library of books with another book of Genesis.

The terms "son of David" and "son of Abraham" become clearer within verses 2–17. It is easy to see why the Messiah is said to be Davidic (David's heir) since the terms "Messiah" (χριστός) and "heir of David" (υἱοῦ Δαυὶδ) were almost synonymous for many people whereby the paradigm of Messiah typically derives from King David (see Matt 22:42). The title, "heir of Abraham" forms an unusual pair with "heir of David." The effect "locates David and his successor within the fuller history of the chosen people."[6] In other words, it situates David within the context of Abraham such that David himself is seen to be derivative of Abraham. The pattern continues within the lineage itself.

All five references to David appearing in the first unit of Matthew (vv. 1–17) place David within a wider context—a context which makes David appear not as the ideal model for the Messiah. David is not simply the feature on display but David himself is contextualized. In the second and third references to David (v. 6) David appears as the culmination of the first stage of ancestry and the beginning of the second stage. The epithet "the king" identifies the first transition point or "culmination point" in which David is both the product of an Abrahamic lineage and the producer of the next stage of the lineage. The third mention of David seems somewhat

---

5. The title, Γένεσις, was already being used for the book of Genesis. Davies and Allison, Jr., *A Critical and Exegetical Commentary*, 151.

6. France, *The Gospel of Matthew*, 35.

honorable (producer of Solomon) yet at the same time it is disgraceful since, according to verse 6, David produced Solomon from another man's wife. So this third reference to David does not highlight David's finest moment but rather David's flaws. This occurs at a point in the genealogy which we might otherwise have assumed to be a high point yet it presents the undoing of David as the beginning of the end of Davidic rule.

Likewise, the fourth and fifth references to David (v. 17) again present David in a wider context as both a culminating role (as the end product of Abraham) and then as the producer of a line of kings (which resulted in the exile to Babylon). According to verse 17, part of the Davidic legacy is revealed to be exile since Abraham led to David and David led to exile.

So the fifth reference to David is not so glamorous (the context of exile); the fourth reference puts David in the context of Abraham; the third reference is couched in disgrace (as a sign portending the downfall of Davidic rule); and both the second and first references to David put David in the context of Abraham.

To conclude that the Messiah is simply the heir of David would be to overlook how David is presented throughout the first seventeen verses. The double title ("son of David son of Abraham") assists in tempering any inclination to see the Messiah simply as a new David. David's kingship itself derives from Abraham. Likewise, Jesus, later, refutes the idea that the Messiah is simply made in the mould of David, instead suggesting a role greater than David's (Matt 22:45). According to Matt 1:17, Jesus's position as the Messiah emerges from a complex heritage which includes exile. In other words, the three stages of development within the lineage indicate that what emerged in the case of David's kingship was imperfect and somewhat responsible for bringing the Babylonian exile. If anything, the Messiah comes to rectify his Davidic heritage and the Davidic legacy, not to replicate it.

While Jesus may not be completely like David, Jesus's unofficial position starts out like David's in the sense that David's early career, after David's "anointment," was not publically (politically) recognized as such (1 Samuel 16). Likewise, when Jesus's life begins, he is not initially recognized by the population in Judea to be inheriting an official leadership position in any way (other families in Bethlehem mentioned in Matthew 2 could also claim a Davidic heritage so the birth of another son in Bethlehem does not automatically cause the locals to suppose that Jesus is "son of David" the Messiah). Apparently, knowledge of Jesus's anointed status does not derive from humans but from heaven; such knowledge is being shared with the audience by the writer of the text. Matthew 1 is consciously written as if revealing a divine perspective, by providing a sacred story of Jesus's chosenness. Like Abraham and David, Jesus is chosen by God to play a specific role.

By verse 17 there are several opportunities to see the complex role that Jesus as the next anointed leader will play. In the second unit, Jesus's status as the final heir is reiterated (in verse 18 a similar heading concerning the Messiah's progeneration appears). In verse 21 his mission is clearly stated as a rescue mission not from outside enemies but from the internal sins of the nation. By verse 25 (by the end of the second unit), we know how Jesus has received his name and so his mission has been declared and he has legally become the son of "Joseph son of David." We would not say, however, that the whole of verse 1 is made fully clear by the end of Matthew 1, especially if we are waiting for Jesus to actually do something in his messianic role.

In summary, the opening verse identifies the protagonist in a providentially-shaped story concerning the making of the Messiah before plotting this within an ancestral lineage. The lineage itself is suitably characterized as Davidic and Abrahamic (the ultimate heir is "of David and of Abraham," namely chosen providentially in God's plan to play a role, like David and Abraham were). Verse 17 further identifies this lineage/storyline as passing through exile as though the emerging chosen leader is also heir to something "exilic." Perhaps he will participate in or address exile and its causes (or facilitate another kind of exile in the final chapter of Matthew by sending his remaining eleven men out into the non-Jewish nations). The lineage is considered a sacred story which operates on a providential timeline to bring the ultimate heir. The labels "son of David" and "son of Abraham" are suggestive of the significance of the mission being introduced. Jesus's arrival is providential in accord with the providential nature of the kind of lineage. The lineage is presented as a three-part story in which Jesus's arrival is seen to be the logical result. The kind of lineage anticipates the kind of Messiah arriving.

Understanding how the lineage is framed in verses 2–16 assists in understanding that the lineage is not particularly focused on introducing Jesus's biological ancestry but rather it is more interested in introducing his mission, identity, and legacy as a continuation of a backstory that is paradigmatic for introducing the life of Jesus. Heritage is one aspect of his "coming-to-be" (γένεσις). Other aspects include his "life disposition" and "legacy."

In other words, the messianic storyline (γένεσις) provides a trajectory for the kind of chosen leader whose life will reflect and address a biblical heritage and will significantly influence the lives of his people.

3

The Messianic Lineage in Matt 1:2–16

Overview

This chapter identifies what is, and is not, in the lineage. There is no variety of verbs, only the one verb repeated for every heir "produced" even in the case of the final heir who "was produced" (using the passive form of the same verb). The references to mothers are apparently meant to explicate Jesus's lineage. In the five cases when mothers are included they are not included as co-producers and so the focus remains on the fathers by inviting readers and hearers to compare the highlighted paternities.

Greek-English Diglot (Matt 1:2–16)

---

2 Ἀβραὰμ ἐγέννησεν τὸν Ἰσαάκ, Ἰσαὰκ δὲ ἐγέννησεν τὸν Ἰακώβ, Ἰακὼβ δὲ ἐγέννησεν τὸν Ἰούδαν καὶ τοὺς ἀδελφοὺς αὐτοῦ, 3 Ἰούδας δὲ ἐγέννησεν τὸν Φαρὲς καὶ τὸν Ζάρα ἐκ τῆς Θαμάρ, Φαρὲς δὲ ἐγέννησεν τὸν Ἐσρώμ, Ἐσρὼμ δὲ ἐγέννησεν τὸν Ἀράμ, 4 Ἀρὰμ δὲ ἐγέννησεν τὸν Ἀμιναδάβ, Ἀμιναδὰβ δὲ ἐγέννησεν τὸν Ναασσών, Ναασσὼν δὲ ἐγέννησεν τὸν Σαλμών, 5 Σαλμὼν δὲ ἐγέννησεν τὸν Βόες ἐκ τῆς Ῥαχάβ, Βόες δὲ ἐγέννησεν τὸν Ἰωβὴδ ἐκ τῆς Ῥούθ, Ἰωβὴ δὲ ἐγέννησεν τὸν Ἰεσσαί, 6 Ἰεσσαὶ δὲ ἐγέννησεν τὸν Δαυὶδ τὸν βασιλέα.

Abraham progenerated Isaac; Isaac progenerated Jacob; Jacob progenerated Judah and his brothers; Judah progenerated Perez and Zerah from Tamar; Perez progenerated Esrom; Esrom progenerated Aram; Aram progenerated Aminadab; Aminadab progenerated Nashon; Nashon progenerated Salmon; Salmon progenerated Boaz from Rahab; Boaz progenerated Obed from Ruth; Obed progenerated Jessie; Jessie progenerated David the king.

Greek-English Diglot (Matt 1:2–16)

Δαυὶδ δὲ ἐγέννησεν τὸν Σολομῶνα ἐκ τῆς τοῦ Οὐρίου, 7 Σολομὼν δὲ ἐγέννησεν τὸν Ῥοβοάμ, Ῥοβοὰμ δὲ ἐγέννησεν τὸν Ἀβιά, Ἀβιὰ δὲ ἐγέννησεν τὸν Ἀσάφ, 8 Ἀσὰφ δὲ ἐγέννησεν τὸν Ἰωσαφάτ, Ἰωσαφὰτ δὲ ἐγέννησεν τὸν Ἰωράμ, Ἰωρὰμ δὲ ἐγέννησεν τὸν Ὀζίαν, 9 Ὀζίας δὲ ἐγέννησεν τὸν Ἰωαθάμ, Ἰωαθὰμ δὲ ἐγέννησεν τὸν Ἀχάζ, Ἀχὰζ δὲ ἐγέννησεν τὸν Ἑζεκίαν, 10 Ἑζεκίας δὲ ἐγέννησεν τὸν Μανασσῆ, Μανασσῆς δὲ ἐγέννησεν τὸν Ἀμώς, Ἀμὼς δὲ ἐγέννησεν τὸν Ἰωσίαν, 11 Ἰωσίας δὲ ἐγέννησεν τὸν Ἰεχονίαν καὶ τοὺς ἀδελφοὺς αὐτοῦ ἐπὶ τῆς μετοικεσίας Βαβυλῶνος.

David progenerated Solomon from her of Uriah; Solomon progenerated Roboam; Roboam progenerated Abiah; Abiah progenerated Asaph; Asaph progenerated Josaphat; Josaphat progenerated Joram; Joram progenerated Uzziah; Uzziah progenerated Jotham; Jotham progenerated Ahaz; Ahaz progenerated Hezekiah; Hezekiah progenerated Manasseh; Manasseh progenerated Amos; Amos progenerated Josiah; Josiah progenerated Jechoniah and his brothers at the time of the exile to Babylon.

12 Μετὰ δὲ τὴν μετοικεσίαν Βαβυλῶνος Ἰεχονίας ἐγέννησεν τὸν Σαλαθιήλ, Σαλαθιὴλ δὲ ἐγέννησεν τὸν Ζοροβαβέλ, 13 Ζοροβαβὲλ δὲ ἐγέννησεν τὸν Ἀβιούδ, Ἀβιοὺδ δὲ ἐγέννησεν τὸν Ἐλιακίμ, Ἐλιακὶμ δὲ ἐγέννησεν τὸν Ἀζώρ, 14 Ἀζὼρ δὲ ἐγέννησεν τὸν Σαδώκ, Σαδὼκ δὲ ἐγέννησεν τὸν Ἀχίμ, Ἀχὶμ δὲ ἐγέννησεν τὸν Ἐλιούδ, 15 Ἐλιοὺδ δὲ ἐγέννησεν τὸν Ἐλεάζαρ, Ἐλεάζαρ δὲ ἐγέννησεν τὸν Ματθάν, Ματθὰν δὲ ἐγέννησεν τὸν Ἰακώβ, 16 Ἰακὼβ δὲ ἐγέννησεν τὸν Ἰωσὴφ τὸν ἄνδρα Μαρίας, ἐξ ἧς ἐγεννήθη Ἰησοῦς ὁ λεγόμενος χριστός. (SBLGNT)

After the exile to Babylon, Jechoniah progenerated Salathiel; Salathiel progenerated Zorobabbel; Zorobabbel progenerated Abiud; Abiud progenerated Eliakim; Eliakim progenerated Azor; Azor progenerated Zadok; Zadok progenerated Achim; Achim progenerated Eliud; Eliud progenerated Eliazar; Eliazar progenerated Matthan; Matthan progenerated Jacob; Jacob progenerated Joseph the husband of Mary from her was progenerated Jesus the one called Messiah.

WHAT IS AND IS not mentioned in verses 2 to 16 is worth observing. There is no variety of verbs, just the one repeated verb (from γεννάω). The verb ἐγέννησεν ("he produced") is used for every heir produced except in the final case where the passive form of the verb is used for Jesus who "was produced" (ἐγεννήθη). So heirs are not simply listed as names but are narrated within a linear series of productions. In this way, every heir in this messianic storyline is said to be produced by the preceding patriarchal figure except for Joseph's heir who is already produced (passively). Yet even here the same verb is used in the passive form ("Jesus was produced" ἐγεννήθη Ἰησοῦς). Only five mothers are mentioned (Tamar, Rahab, Ruth, Uriah's [woman], and Mary).

Verses 2–16 present a messianic γένεσις in the form of a father-to-son lineage (usually labeled a "patrilineal genealogy"). The entire γένεσις consists of a core "father produced son" formula along with several additional annotations in which the basic formula is extended or modified. Some of these annotations mark off the three-part timeline, namely the epithet "the king" (τὸν βασιλέα) culminates the first group in verse 6; the second group culminates in verse 11 with a reference to the ordeal of the deported royal family along with other elite families to Babylon (καὶ τοὺς ἀδελφοὺς αὐτοῦ ἐπὶ τῆς μετοικεσίας Βαβυλῶνος); the third group culminates in verse 16 with the epithet "the one said to be the Messiah" (ὁ λεγόμενος χριστός).

The five additional references to mothers represent the most number of any one kind of annotation as though forming a group or a major pattern which is why I list them separately from the other various annotations.

Greek-English Diglot for the Annotations (Matt 1:3–16)

v. 2	καὶ τοὺς ἀδελφοὺς αὐτοῦ	and his brothers
v. 3	καὶ τὸν Ζάρα	and Zerah
v. 6	τὸν βασιλέα	the king
v. 11	καὶ τοὺς ἀδελφοὺς αὐτοῦ	and his brothers
v. 11	ἐπὶ τῆς μετοικεσίας Βαβυλῶνος	at the deportation to Babylon
v. 12	μετὰ δὲ τὴν μετοικεσίαν Βαβυλῶνος	after the deportation to Babylon
v. 16	τὸν ἄνδρα	the husband
v. 16	ὁ λεγόμενος χριστός	the one called Messiah

The Five References to Mothers

v. 3	ἐκ τῆς Θαμάρ	from Tamar
v. 5	ἐκ τῆς Ῥαχάβ	from Rahab
v. 5	ἐκ τῆς Ῥούθ	from Ruth
v. 6	ἐκ τῆς τοῦ Οὐρίου	from her of Uriah
v. 16	Μαρίας, ἐξ ἧς	of Mary, from her

The references to mothers occur in the fourth, tenth, and eleventh heir productions by adding "from" + "name of mother" while in the fifteenth heir production the addition is "from" + "of" + "name of husband." In the fortieth (final) heir production, the reference to a mother uses the genitive relative pronoun rather than genitive definite article and uses a modified word order. In this case, the would-be progenitor is still mentioned first but the mention of heir and mother is reversed so that the mother is mentioned before the heir ("name of progenitor" + "name of mother" + "from her" + "was progenerated"). A further difference in the final heir production is the addition of "the husband of" inserted between Joseph and Mary since the active role of progeneration for Joseph has been removed. Joseph is succinctly introduced as the product of his father Jacob and simultaneously as the husband of the mother of his heir. Joseph is not identified as the one who produced his heir so he is simply the one married to the mother of his heir.[1]

In other words, the word order in the final case has been rearranged so that the name of the final heir can be mentioned last (with the added epithet "the one said to be the Messiah") highlighting Jesus as the final heir in the lineage along with his messianic title. Also, it might easily have omitted referring to Mary by instead saying, "Jacob produced Joseph for whom Jesus was produced." Taking all this into consideration, the additional mention of "from Mary" is more similar to the previous four references than it might seem.

Having the final heir as the grammatical subject means that the passive verb applies to Jesus who "from Mary was begotten." Yet using the active version of the verb for what previous patriarchs "gave birth to" seems to credit the fathers with too much. One reason for using the same verb is to resemble the noun "progeneration" ($\gamma \acute{\epsilon} \nu \epsilon \sigma \iota \varsigma$) in verse 1 so that the Messiah's progeneration culminates a long series (or story) of progenerations. The vocabulary throughout verses 2–16 is intentionally limited so as to keep the topic of "progeneration" in focus.

The annotations to the formula can be thought of as additional comments that highlight something noteworthy. Some mothers are included in the narration yet they are only included within the pattern of their partner's progenerating which means that the inclusion of the mothers does

---

1. Nolland notes, "The language created a detour around this pattern in a manner which would normally be considered a distinction without a difference." Nolland, *Gospel of Matthew*, 85.

not affect the form of the verb used. To use the case of Boaz and Ruth as an example, the inclusion of Ruth might, in theory, have affected the verb so as to become plural and instead say, "Boaz and Ruth produced Obed" (Βόες καὶ δέ Ῥούθ ἐγέννησαν τὸν Ἰωβὴδ). Yet that is not what it says. Instead, it says, "Boaz produced Obed from Ruth" (Βόες δὲ ἐγέννησεν τὸν Ἰωβὴδ ἐκ τῆς Ῥούθ) keeping the verb singular (ἐγέννησεν "he produced"). So even when mothers are mentioned, they are not included as grammatical subjects of the production. One mother, Bathsheba, is left unnamed, referred to only as "her of Uriah."

In the basic formula, fathers are producing sons as though by themselves. The formulaic pattern would not be as noticeably odd if left unmodified and only mentioned patriarchs throughout. However, the first addition of a named mother in verse 3 along with the four other references to mothers makes the basic formula of patriarchal productions without mothers seem odd by comparison. The lack of mothers from the beginning suddenly seems strange when references to some mothers occur along the way.

Consequently, the idea that some fathers are said to have gained their sons *from mothers* (mothers who are not identified as co-producers of the heirs) invites further explanation. The lack of subjectivity for the mothers has the effect of calling even more attention to the patriarchal nature of what the fathers are doing (or not doing in the case of Joseph), namely *Judah* produced Perez and Zerah from Tamar; *Salmon* produced Boaz from Rahab; *Boaz* produced Obed from Ruth; *David* produced Solomon from her of Uriah; and Jesus was produced from Mary (and *not*, apparently, by Joseph).

It will be helpful to compare how the repeated formula is functioning *without* mothers and how the added modifications are functioning *with* mothers.

The progression of ancestry does not leave much room for an audience to consider the processes at work when only the basic formula is used ("Abraham produced Isaac; Isaac produced Jacob . . ."). But when the additional modifications to the basic formula appear, particular elements in the narrated ancestry are highlighted. This has the effect of slowing down the rapid progression of heir productions and encourages further consideration of the processes by which the ancestry progresses (see further chapter 8, "How Matt 1:18–25 Completes Matt 1:1–17").

Reading with the text would suggest focusing on what was going on with those patriarchs whose acquisition of heirs is highlighted. Apparently, the text is not inviting readers and hearers to form an opinion about the women.

The usual approach has been for commentators to talk about what they think of these women or to look for similarities among these women and their behaviors. Such an approach eventually leads many scholars to a point where any negative criticism of these women is allayed and the mothers are praised.[2]

According to Matthew 1, commentators were not necessarily expected to offer an opinion on the women in the first place. Instead, the focus is on what Judah, Salmon, Boaz, David, and Joseph did or did not do (namely "progenerate" their heirs).

Although the invitation to compare Joseph's paternity with the previous four highlighted fathers has not previously been studied, I would like to call attention to the following nine quotations in which it would appear as though scholars have already acknowledged the essential argument of the present book (I cite them together as a group):

> All four women were connected to other men than the father of their child.[3]

> The patriarchal figure [of Joseph] constructed by significant intertextuality is deconstructed by the text."[4]

> Men, it seems, are the principal protagonists of Israel's history, and women function only as a means by which their male counterparts secure their futures. Yet it is precisely this idea that is undermined by the text.[5]

---

2. Warner concludes, "The women were 'tainted . . . in the eyes of the world . . . but . . . righteous in the eyes of God." Warner, "Uncertain Women," 25. Likewise Scott, "Yet despite this shame, these women all have the honor ascribed to them by the Lord." Scott, "The Birth of the Reader," 88. Higgins sees the pattern extending to Jesus, "[T]hey have an appearance of immorality but when you investigate those situations they are actually women of great virtue . . . [similarly] the things that Jesus does have the appearance of sinfulness to some but they are actually the greatest acts of holiness; they have the same moral shape as the women in the genealogy." Higgins, "The Hidden Virtue of Women," 6:31–8:25.

3. Klip, *Biblical Genealogies*, 310.

4. Wainwright, "Rachel Weeping for Her Children," 464.

5. Weren, *Studies in Matthew's Gospel*, 115.

Basically, the genealogy supports and subverts ancient hegemonic constructions of masculinity . . . by pointing out their [the highlighted men's] flaws.[6]

In short, Joseph shows up his inferior, inelastic forefathers by acting in rather un-masculine fashion.[7]

The accusation of improper sexual conduct [by Judah] is explicit in the case of Tamar, implicit in the case of Rahab, avoided in Ruth's case by the secrecy of Boaz, and leveled against David in Bathsheba's case.[8]

Judah without a further reflection asked for Tamar to be "burnt at the stake" and only later, when he became aware of his role in the case, declared her "the righteous" (Gen 38:26). David gave a death penalty verdict to the rich offender in 2 Sam 12:5–6 and realizing he was a guilty man himself in relation to Bathsheba and Uriah acknowledged his guilt (2 Sam 12:5–12). Joseph thought of following the provision of the law with regard to Mary but in a more humane way by not exposing her to public ridicule.[9]

In all cases, the men face a challenge to their sexual prowess. And in all cases . . . "normal" procreation is irrelevant if not a nuisance . . . The genealogy continues to suggest a line of undesiring sires. Rahab . . . evokes the visiting spies who do not avail themselves of the services of the brothel . . . Boaz shows no interest in procreation . . . David has no desire that Bathsheba become pregnant . . . The men with whom the Matthean women are paired (either in the genealogy itself or in the background stories) are those who did not want or, at the least, had no expressed interest in, the women with whom they are paired to have children. The same applies to Joseph, who seeks to divorce the pregnant Mary. The genealogy can be read as promoting celibacy (a Matthean interest), even as it undermines the value of both marriage and procreation in wedlock, the two major elements of patriarchal society.[10]

In addition to the names of the messianic mothers, which are presented in Matthew 1, I suggest that the "Davidic impregnation type-scene" influenced the Gospels' authors. In the biblical pattern, all [these particular] men in the Davidic lineage are

6. Doane, "Masculinities of the Husbands," 91–101.

7. Spencer, "Those Riotous—Yet Righteous—Foremothers," 26.

8. Schaberg, "Feminist Interpretations," 27 n59.

9. Naseri, "The Four OT Women," 21.

10. Levine, "Women's Humor," 121–22.

described in similar terms as unknowing ("and he did not know when she lay down or when she rose," Genesis 19:33–35, and also slightly differently in Genesis 38:16 and Ruth 3:14).[11]

The above quotes seem to betray more knowledge than the sources of these quotations intended. In their original contexts, the topic is left open-ended and hypothetical as though the idea of comparing the fathers and their paternities is just an interesting thought. As far as I can tell, the above tantalizing collection of quotes exhausts the analysis of the topic as previously studied. Even Doane's essay, which compares the highlighted fathers, does not study the pattern that the audience would be expected to notice (how the five fathers gained their respective paternities according to their representation in Matthew 1).

Recently, scholars have embarked on "masculinity studies" so as to expose and critique the gendered nature of texts such as Matthew 1 from a modern vantage point.[12] Yet Matthew 1 already got there, by first offering its own study on the topic. By intentionally highlighting the patriarchal topic of how five patriarchs became fathers, Matthew 1 offers its own study in patriarchy.

This should not be so surprising when we consider that the text comments on itself in Matthew 1 in verse 17 and in verse 22. At these points the writer's perspective of the account being written is revealed more directly. We could say that it is the written persona of a "narrator" who is revealing a narrator's stance in relation to the narrative. At such points the text's own "point of view" is most explicit.[13] The text's own annotations can be considered narratorial comments in which the five references to mothers suggest something of the narrator's critical perspective for evaluating heir productions in Matthew 1.

In other words, the references to mothers are narratorial comments pointing out something comparable about the relationships had by five fathers in the process of gaining their heirs. These comments suggest a critical perspective operating from *within* the text.

11. Kaniel, "Myth of the Messianic Mother," 100.

12. Glessner states the goal as "exposing and destabilizing the machinery underlying the gender(ed) power structures embedded in this ancient text." Glessner, "On 'Being a Just Man,'" 127.

13. Resseguie refers to Robert Alter's "scale of means" whereby a narrator's comments are at the top of the scale for how to evaluate the story. Resseguie, *Narrative Criticism*, 130–31.

In summary, the lineage charts a providentially guided three-stage progression leading to a final figure of an ideal leader in the arrival of the Messiah himself. The lineage is not presented as a list of names since every single heir production (of a male heir) is narrated with the same verb of "production." The repeated father-produced-son formula is only slightly modified for the final heir so as to be in the passive form ("was produced") so as to bypass Joseph's active role whilst maintaining the same verb. Occasionally some mothers are mentioned but the verb remains in the singular form as though to comment on the patriarch's paternity meaning that no mother is included within the grammatical subject of the verb. Also Uriah is named whilst Bathsheba is "Uriah's [woman]." The cumulative effect calls attention to what the fathers are doing (or not doing as in the case of Joseph). It seems to be written this way so as to highlight the issue of comparative paternities in the patriarchs' acquisition of their heirs.

It will be easier to see exactly how this theme works after having first looked at some other patterns in Matthew 1. It will be helpful to unpack the second part of Matthew 1 by beginning with those elements that are commonly assumed to belong to the story in order to clarify what the text is and is not suggesting we infer about Mary's unexpected baby, namely Joseph's unexpected acquisition of Jesus as his heir. Then we can more easily compare this with the previously highlighted cases.

4

Looking For Things Not There
in Matt 1:18–25

Overview

This chapter looks at the assumptions commonly read into Matt 1:18–25. Most assumptions have in common the idea that the text is inviting us to think about what exactly happened (historically/biologically) when Mary *conceived* or what Joseph and others thought about Mary's conception. The five most popular assumptions concern: conception; scandalous rumors; forbidden premarital sex; potential execution; and assumed adultery. It is commonly thought that reading such things into the text helps the text to make sense yet these things are not necessarily compatible with what is in the text. In fact, much of what is commonly imposed on Matt 1:18–25 is unhelpful and reflects the assumptions of commentators rather than of the text.

Greek-English Diglot (Matt 1:18–25)

Τοῦ δὲ Ἰησοῦ χριστοῦ ἡ γένεσις οὕτως ἦν. μνηστευθείσης τῆς μητρὸς αὐτοῦ Μαρίας τῷ Ἰωσήφ, πρὶν ἢ συνελθεῖν αὐτοὺς εὑρέθη ἐν γαστρὶ ἔχουσα ἐκ πνεύματος ἁγίου. Ἰωσὴφ δὲ ὁ ἀνὴρ αὐτῆς, δίκαιος ὢν καὶ μὴ θέλων αὐτὴν δειγματίσαι, ἐβουλήθη λάθρα ἀπολῦσαι αὐτήν. ταῦτα δὲ αὐτοῦ ἐνθυμηθέντος ἰδοὺ ἄγγελος κυρίου κατ' ὄναρ ἐφάνη αὐτῷ λέγων· Ἰωσὴφ υἱὸς Δαυίδ, μὴ φοβηθῇς παραλαβεῖν Μαρίαν τὴν γυναῖκά σου, τὸ γὰρ ἐν αὐτῇ γεννηθὲν ἐκ πνεύματός ἐστιν ἁγίου· τέξεται δὲ υἱὸν καὶ καλέσεις τὸ ὄνομα αὐτοῦ Ἰησοῦν, αὐτὸς γὰρ σώσει τὸν λαὸν αὐτοῦ ἀπὸ τῶν ἁμαρτιῶν αὐτῶν. τοῦτο δὲ ὅλον γέγονεν ἵνα πληρωθῇ τὸ ῥηθὲν ὑπὸ κυρίου διὰ τοῦ προφήτου λέγοντος· Ἰδοὺ ἡ παρθένος ἐν γαστρὶ ἕξει καὶ τέξεται υἱόν, καὶ καλέσουσιν τὸ ὄνομα αὐτοῦ Ἐμμανουήλ· ὅ ἐστιν μεθερμηνευόμενον Μεθ' ἡμῶν ὁ θεός. ἐγερθεὶς δὲ ὁ Ἰωσὴφ ἀπὸ τοῦ ὕπνου ἐποίησεν ὡς προσέταξεν αὐτῷ ὁ ἄγγελος κυρίου καὶ παρέλαβεν τὴν γυναῖκα αὐτοῦ· καὶ οὐκ ἐγίνωσκεν αὐτὴν ἕως οὗ ἔτεκεν υἱόν· καὶ ἐκάλεσεν τὸ ὄνομα αὐτοῦ Ἰησοῦν. (SBLGNT)

The Jesus-Messiah's progeneration was this way. His mother Mary, being betrothed to Joseph, without yet being united, already had a pregnant belly from the Holy Spirit. Joseph, her husband, being righteous, and not wanting to shame her, decided he would quietly divorce her. Having resolved to do these things, behold an angel of the Lord appeared to him in a dream saying, "Joseph Son of David, do not fear to take Mary, your wife. For the one progenerated in her is from the Holy Spirit; she will give birth to a son; you will call his name Jesus; for he will save his people from their sins." This whole thing took place so that what was spoken by the Lord through the prophet would be filled up (saying): "Behold the virgin will have a pregnant belly; she will give birth to a son; they will call his name Emmanuel', which means 'God is with us.'" Rising from sleep, Joseph did what he was told to do by the angel of the Lord. He took his wife. He had no sexual intimacy with her prior to the time she gave birth to a son. He called his name Jesus.

THOUGH NUMEROUS THINGS ARE mentioned in verses 18–25, commentators have tended to prefer reading other things into Matt 1:18–25 concerning: (1) conception; (2) scandalous rumors; (3) forbidden premarital sex; (4) expected execution; and (5) assumed adultery.

Each assumption will be examined according to three questions:

- Is it mentioned in the text?

- Is it compatible with the text?

- What reason might we want to hold this assumption?

Conception

Many of us automatically import the idea of conception into the text, thinking that the story requires it in order to make sense. It is commonly assumed that Matt 1:18–25 tells of Mary becoming pregnant miraculously/virginally from the Holy Spirit. We can examine this assumption according to the text in Matthew 1 without mixing in what is said about Jesus's origins in Luke or John. This is especially worthwhile if neither Luke nor John were yet published at the time Matthew was first published.

It is reasonable to suppose that Joseph's production of his own heir, in Matthew 1, is entirely replaced with God's production of an heir for Joseph. Yet we might consider the various possible ways this idea might be working according to Matthew 1.

Is miraculous conception mentioned in the text? The idea of Mary becoming pregnant miraculously from the Holy Spirit is only partially mentioned in the text. The part mentioned is that Mary's pregnancy is identified as being "from the Holy Spirit," which is mentioned twice (in verse 18: "her having a belly from the Holy Spirit"; and in verse 20: "the child in her is from the Holy Spirit.") The Holy Spirit is clearly identified as responsible for what is *presently* the case, namely Mary is expecting a child (v. 18) and what is *about to happen*, namely Mary will be giving birth to the Messiah (v. 20).

Notice, however, that the other "half" of the assumption is not mentioned in the text, namely that Mary *became* pregnant. Oddly, from our perspective, there is no mention of Mary *becoming* pregnant. Verse 18 does not say Mary *became pregnant* from the Holy Spirit but says that Mary's pregnancy from the Holy Spirit *became evident*. The verb refers to Mary *already being* pregnant when the story begins. Naturally, we might want to take it as implied that Mary must have initially *become* pregnant at some earlier point in time in order for her now to *be* pregnant. Yet, even though we could think about that point in time, that point in time is not mentioned in the story.

Likewise, the second reference to the Holy Spirit in verse 20 does not say that Mary's child *was produced from* the Holy Spirit; it says, "the produced-one [the child], within Mary, is from the Holy Spirit."

Considering the various events mentioned, it seems worthwhile observing that the story twice misses an opportunity to mention Mary *becoming* pregnant.

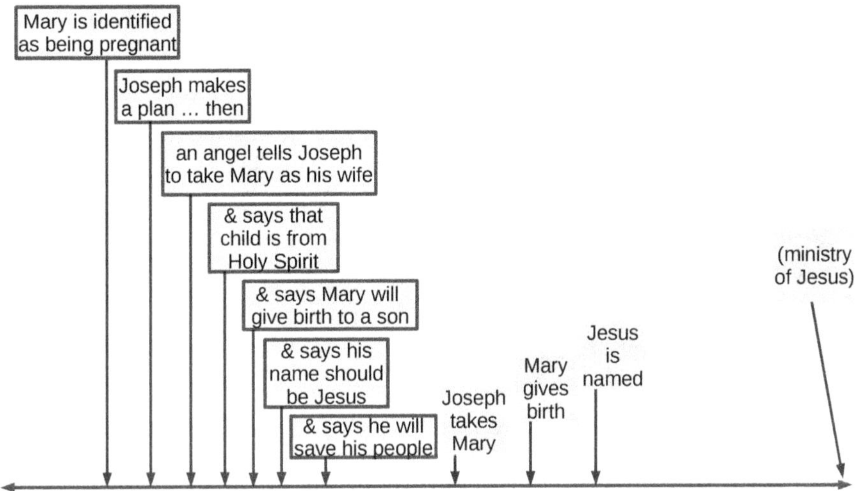

Figure 2. Sequence of mentioned events.

The mention, in verse 20, that Mary's child "from the spirit is holy" (ἐκ πνεύματός ἐστιν ἁγίου) does not speak of a "past" event but of a concurrent event with future ramifications. It asserts the significance of the child for the future as "the born one."[1] It is "the heir in her" being spoken of within the context of a prophecy in which the following three elements ("she will give birth . . . you will name . . . he will save . . .") are all future oriented. Fittingly, all four elements of the prophetic birth speak of the significance of "the born one" by focusing on the future.

There is a potential reference to conception by implication in the prophetic quotation in verse 23 which mentions "the virgin" (ἡ παρθένος) who "will have a [pregnant] belly" (ἐν γαστρὶ ἕξει). Mention of "the virgin" is the clearest indication that Mary might be seen to be pregnant in the same manner as that indicated in the quotation in verse 23 as though Mary were "the virgin," since Mary, by implication, is like "the virgin" in the quotation who "will have a [pregnant] belly." Though verses 18–25 never directly refer to Mary herself as "the virgin," the language of pregnancy used in verse 23 is the same as that used for Mary's pregnancy in verse 18 ("having a [pregnant] belly" ἐν γαστρὶ ἔχουσα). In Mary's case it is a pregnancy "from the

1. Similarly, Toan Do (associate of the Nida School of Translation Studies) translates τὸ γὰρ ἐν αὐτῇ γεννηθὲν as "the one to be born in her." Do, *What Jesus Says*, 178.

Holy Spirit" (ἐκ πνεύματος ἁγίου) and in the case of verse 23 it refers to the expecting mother as "the virgin" (ἡ παρθένος, being the same term used for the expecting mother in the Greek version of Isa 7:14).

In the case of verse 23, there is "the virgin" who will *be* pregnant at some point which is something noteworthy or unexpected. This sounds very similar to verse 18's description of that point in time in which Mary is "found" to *be* pregnant. Mary's pregnant belly *becoming* evident apparently suits the assertion that "Behold! The virgin will have a pregnant belly" (Ἰδοὺ ἡ παρθένος ἐν γαστρὶ ἕξει). Like Mary's pregnancy, "the virgin" spoken about in verse 23 is spoken of as "having" not "conceiving" a pregnancy.[2]

The significance of the pregnancy in verse 23 is not about the kind of conception but about the fulfillment of a prophetic annunciation. That is, the prophetic speech is itself something noteworthy and the naming of the born child is significant for those who perceive God's attending presence among the people. In the original context of Isa 7:14, the "sign" given is the entire birth annunciation "including the pregnancy, birth, and the child's name."[3] The pregnancy and birth that the virgin will have (in Isaiah) and the pregnancy and birth that Mary now already has (in Matthew) both anticipate a significant result for the people as a sign that God is present.

If we choose to take the quoted passage in verse 23 as referring to a miraculous conception then we are likely to assume the same for Mary's pregnancy since Mary's pregnancy is clearly parallel. But we might also understand the significance of saying, "the virgin will be pregnant," as a series of narrated steps ("then she will be [noticeably] pregnant" as with Mary in verse 18). We may or may not take "having a pregnant belly" as synonymous to "becoming pregnant" (conceive) so we may or may not infer a miracle or even a reference to conception.

We might compare the child to be born "from Mary" with an earlier mentioned child in the genealogy born "from Ruth." The book of Ruth presents both sexual production of a child *and* holy conception. According to the book of Ruth, the anticipated child about to be produced is presented as being from a woman and simultaneously sanctioned by God. In Ruth 4:12, the elders say to Boaz, "And may your house be like the house of Perez, whom Tamar bore to Judah from the seed that the

2. "Being pregnant" is not necessarily the same as "getting pregnant." The Greek for "she is going to become pregnant" ("she will conceive") would be ἐν γαστρὶ λήψεται or ἐν γαστρὶ συλλήψεται. This is noted also by Nolland, "ἐν γαστρὶ ἔχειν is concerned with being pregnant rather than becoming pregnant." Nolland, *Gospel of Matthew*, 94.

3. Hamori, "Heavenly Bodies," 491.

LORD will give to you from this young woman." Here the offspring is spoken of as being both "from God" and "from this girl" (and likened to Tamar's progeny). The idea of conception is then reemphasized when, in the following verse, it says that God gave Ruth "conception" (κύησις/הֵרָיוֹן) "and he [Boaz] was sexually united with her and the Lord gave to her conception"). Ruth 4:13 presents "the only conception formulation in the Hebrew Bible where YHWH gives conception to the woman.[4] The child Obed is the result of sexual union and divine assistance such that the child is divinely sanctioned from conception. Similarly, in Matthew 1, Jesus is the child who is "from Mary" and "from the Holy Spirit" except that conception is absent in Matt 1:16, 18, and 20.

Is miraculous conception compatible with the text? In short, miraculous conception is potentially compatible with the text, with some hesitation. The fact that the text never mentions Mary *becoming* pregnant does not necessarily eliminate the idea that either conception or a miracle is expected to be read into the story. Mary's pregnancy being "from the Holy Spirit" might be compatible with the assumption that the child has been produced, miraculously, by God. Yet it is helpful at this point to acknowledge how we might still arrive at that conclusion by charting the increasing degrees of specificity necessary to make such a conclusion concerning what "from the Holy Spirit" might mean in verses 18 and 20.

The expression "from the Holy Spirit" could be a reference to Mary's pregnancy being something that is known and approved by God, namely that according to God, Mary's pregnancy is considered something good, leading to beneficial results. Or, it could be a reference to God being in charge of (or taking charge of) Mary's pregnancy, such that God has determined the outcome. We could narrow down the options by making increasingly more specific assertions of what it might mean to say that Mary now being pregnant is "from the Holy Spirit."

---

4. Finlay, *Birth Report Genre*, 250, being "the only direct action of YHWH in the entire book of Ruth."

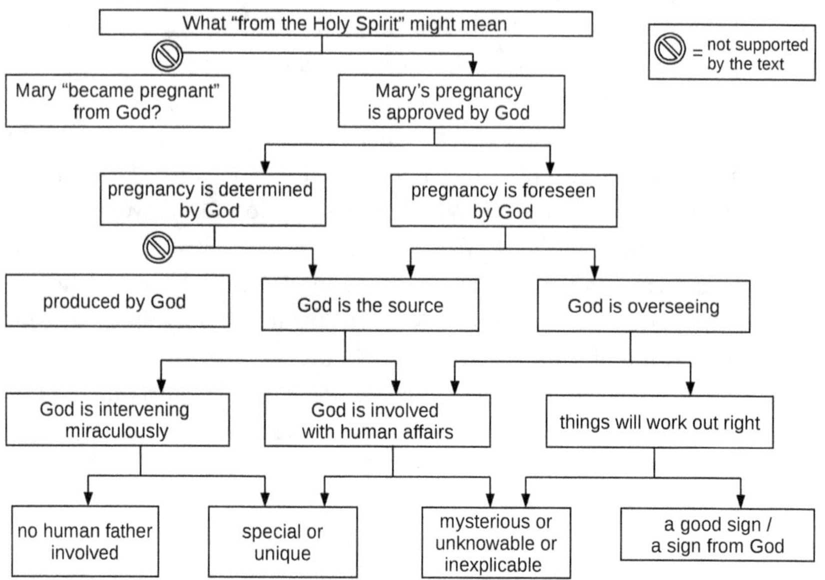

Figure 3. Flowchart for interpreting "from the Holy Spirit."

As seen in figure 3, even though the text does not mention Mary becoming pregnant or that the Holy Spirit produced a child, we might still conclude that a biological/human father was unnecessary for explaining Mary's pregnancy. In fact, considering how ambiguous the phrase is, there are a variety of conclusions we might reach. We might conclude that Mary being pregnant is a unique case or at least is a special case. Or we might conclude that Mary's pregnancy is mysterious, unknowable, or inexplicable. At the far right-hand side we might conclude, more circumspectly, that "from the Holy Spirit" expresses something good is happening or about to happen, as a sign from God of the Holy Spirit's providential involvement in the outcome. The various conclusions are not necessarily mutually exclusive. At minimum, we could say that it reassuringly suggests the opposite of something bad or adverse (compare Paul identifying a couple's child as "holy").[5]

---

5. In 1 Cor 7:14, Paul refers to the offspring of couples in which one spouse is an unbelieving spouse. He reassures them that, in such cases, the children "are holy" (ἅγιά ἐστιν).

Jane Schaberg, even while accepting the term "conception" and embracing the term "begotten," still managed to recognize that the text is not speaking as many of us tend to assume, since the point is that:

> God is the ultimate power of life in this as in all conceptions . . . Is Matthew also speaking about the election of this child from the womb for a role in Israel's history? Clearly yes: Jesus will save his people from their sins (1:21), will be called Emmanuel (1:23). Matthew may also think of the Spirit's role in Jesus' conception as an explanation of his extraordinary career and his final transformation and empowerment . . . This begetting constitutes him Son of God in a special sense, as the one who sums up in his existence the whole history of Israel from Exodus onwards.

For readers unfamiliar with the Greek text it might seem strange that I have not explained "that which has been conceived in her," which is the way many English versions choose to translate the expression in verse 20 (τὸ ἐν αὐτῇ γεννηθὲν). Such a translation does not treat τὸ γεννηθὲν ("the progenerated") as a noun because of the tendency to read it as a reference to conception. An even more extreme reading would be to take it as speaking of "the one conceived by her" which would make it sound even more like it is talking about Mary becoming pregnant. Yet the supposed verb here underlying "conceived" is not a verb for conception nor is it here functioning as a verb since it functions substantively as a noun with its own definite article. It is a repackaged version of the verb used throughout the genealogy to refer to the heirs "produced" in every single case, including Mary's child "produced" or "born" in verse 16. So now, in verse 20, the reference is to that same "heir," namely "the born" or "the child" or "the one produced" (using a neuter adjectival participle form functioning substantively as a noun).[6]

When the angel speaks of "the heir in her" (τὸ ἐν αὐτῇ γεννηθὲν "the in her heir") the angel is speaking of "Mary carrying the heir." By having the words "in her" placed inside "the heir" ("the *in her* heir") it is interesting to consider the effect of such word placement. While, practically speaking, the mother still encompasses the child within her body, linguistically speaking, "the child surrounds the mother" (perhaps even suggesting that "she is

---

6. A similar neuter adjectival form appears in John 3:6 "the offspring of flesh is flesh and the offspring of the spirit is spirit" (τὸ γεγεννημένον ἐκ τῆς σαρκὸς σάρξ ἐστιν, καὶ τὸ γεγεννημένον ἐκ τοῦ πνεύματος πνεῦμά ἐστιν) and 1 John 5:4 "because every heir of God conquers the world" (ὅτι πᾶν τὸ γεγεννημένον ἐκ τοῦ θεοῦ νικᾷ τὸν κόσμον).

being protected by the child").[7] It is as though Mary's status were bound up, literally and literarily, in the status of the child.

The same pattern can be seen in the fourfold structure of the prophecy given by the angel, "*The heir* is from the Holy Spirit; *she* will give birth to a son; *you* will call his name Jesus; *he* will save his people from their sins." That is, the heir appears as both the first and fourth subjects while the parents are put in the middle in second and third places such that the references to the heir surround the parents. It is not simply that the parents give the child an identity but the child gives them theirs.

Though useful, the above flow chart does not differentiate between the two references to Mary's pregnancy (v. 18) and Mary's child (v. 20). The two references are not identical since the first reference is to the "belly" Mary is unexpectedly showing, and the second is to the "child" Mary is providentially carrying. Specifically, the second reference is to the "heir" previously referred to in verse 16 (the final heir, the Messiah himself).

The progression between the first and second subjects is worth pondering. In the first reference it is Mary's pregnant belly that is spoken of as being knowable (or discoverable/seeable). By comparison, in the second reference the angel speaks directly to Joseph concerning the child as if the child is already seeable and knowable from God's perspective. Verse 18 narrates what can be known according to a human perspective, namely a pregnancy. In verse 20 an angel speaks to Joseph of a divine perspective, namely about what God sees (a special child who is the chosen heir Mary is presently carrying within her). The angel speaks as though the child already has an identity known by God, and determined by God, which is immediately clarified to Joseph in the following three clauses (a son; a name; a mission; namely: "Mary will give birth to a son; you will call his name Jesus; for he will save his people from their sins"). God knows the destiny of this child and is endorsing the child to Joseph as "the heir" with a divine mission.

It might seem to us that the idea of Mary having conceived at some earlier point is something that should be included or should be read into the text because it seems compatible with the text. After all, the story is about how the final messianic heir came about. But we should probably consider why the text has twice omitted to mention conception where we might have expected it to be. It is not likely to be an accidental omission. Perhaps we might be more hesitant before reading it (back) into the story. It is helpful to think about the potential reasons for the omission.

7. Duckwitz, *Reading the Gospel*, 11.

Omitted to remain mysterious

By not saying that Mary's child *was produced from* the Holy Spirit it leaves the child's precise origins mysterious as though ascertaining the child's biology is not the point of the story.

Omitted to avoid sounding like impregnation

By not mentioning conception it avoids any reference to male impregnation of Mary. It avoids placing the Holy Spirit in a masculine role as the father/begetter of the child. Otherwise it may have implied male input, as though Mary had been impregnated by divine seed. The reason to avoid any kind of male contribution would mean avoiding sounding like Mary has been impregnated by a god as in Greek mythology, where Greek gods sometimes impregnate human women who in turn give birth to demigods. Similarly, in ancient Jewish mythology there existed a retelling of the story from Genesis 6 in which the story is about rogue, angelic beings who take human wives and produce offspring (these offspring introduce bad things into the world and so cause the flood; see 1 Enoch).

Omitted to indicate there is no human father

The avoidance of any "fathering" language avoids the notion of a father altogether. Specifically, it avoids implying a biological human father. This tends to backfire for readers and hearers because when some of us are told not to think about a biological father we immediately start thinking of a biological father. If the purpose of the story is to avoid it then many of us, ironically, may be inclined to focus on it.

Omitted to indicate outcome not origin

In verse 20, the angel is announcing the child into the world and foretelling the child's destiny or mission. The angel has just spoken a sentence to Joseph instructing him to go ahead with the marriage, and now the angel is speaking the first of four more sentences announcing the child into the world using a typical "annunciation" formula.[8] So it makes sense that the interest,

8. For an examination of the annunciations in Gen 15:1–6; 16:7–14; 17:1–22; 18:1–16;

at least in verse 20, is in the child's future rather than in Mary's past. In other words, the focus is on the providential outcome (the child and the child's destiny) rather than on the cause (how the child originated).

Omitted to avoid sounding invasive to Mary's body

Conception may have been omitted so as to avoid sounding invasive to Mary's body. It may be inappropriate for the narrator to mention it or for the angel to be talking to Joseph about Mary being impregnated in such a way. If instead it were Joseph's body and Joseph were the one having the child then perhaps the angel would have spoken to Joseph differently. Perhaps it is just a more respectful way that the angel is speaking. Note that Mary's child is the subject of verse 20, not Mary.

Omitted to preserve a paternal role for Joseph

If the angel wants to persuade Joseph to step into a paternal role then the angel is setting things up for Joseph. There is a role ready for Joseph to fill. Joseph is being invited to step into that role by being invited to be known as the father. Mention of a previous father might have undermined what the angel was trying to communicate. It would make sense that it would not want to make it sound like that role has already been filled.

In all, the question of whether the idea of conception is compatible with the story vignette has to deal with the many practical reasons for its omission from the story and the fact that the emphasis in the story is elsewhere. It does not seem to be an accident that conception is missing from the story. When the story begins, Mary has already been pregnant for many weeks (perhaps several months). The child is identified as the chosen heir destined to save his people. While not impossible, it is doubtful that the story is written expecting the audience to import unmentioned details imagined from Mary's moment of conception in order to make a point about biology.

Because of the way that the story is predominantly interpreted in commentaries and sermons, I, like many others, feel pressured to have to pick a "side," namely to offer an opinion about what we might infer

----

25:20–23; Judg 13:2–23; 2 Sam 7:4–17; 1 Chr 22:8–10; 1 Kgs 13:1–3; 2 Kgs 4:11–16; and Isa 7:10–17, see Ashmon, *Birth Annunciations*.

about the biology of Mary's child by siding either with those who infer a miraculous virginal conception or those who infer that a biological human father was naturally responsible. This is a more relevant task for those attempting to make assertions about stages of historical events so the pressure to choose is more historical than textual.[9] According to the poetics of verses 18–25, I am not encouraged to draw any firm conclusions on the topic of biological conception.

The best conclusion to draw is that the child to be born from Mary is the Messiah *not* because of his biology. We are not required to work on the biological or historical question to ascertain the child's genetics according to Matthew 1 since Jesus's biology is *not* what made him the Messiah.

Why might we assume that miraculous conception is in the story? It is understandable that many interpreters want to take the hint that Mary might still be considered a virgin *after* she was noticed to be pregnant. It is understandable that many Christians would like to identify Jesus's unique messianic role in terms that express that uniqueness biologically especially when it is difficult not to be influenced by other theological writings in which other writers also make claims or inferences about Jesus's origins. Yet, according to Matthew, Jesus's incorporation into Joseph's ancestral lineage is *not* based on biological reasoning.[10]

People might continue to hold to the assumption that verses 18–25 are talking about conception if they do not notice that conception is absent from the story, especially if they are already familiar with the account of Jesus's conception and birth in the book of Luke. How Mary becomes pregnant from the Holy Spirit *is* an idea present in the Lukan story (Luke 1:34–35). In Luke, the story begins when Mary is not yet pregnant and then just before she becomes pregnant the angel Gabriel informs her that she is about to *become* pregnant and then Mary asks about *how* she will become pregnant. In Luke we find language of how (πῶς) combined with language of conception (συλλήμψῃ ἐν γαστρὶ). Some of us may inadvertently import the idea from Luke 1 into Matthew 1 without noticing that there are no references to conception in Matthew.

Another reason many of us tend to import conception into the text is due to the way we read the story's conclusion. We might think that the notion

---

9. Lincoln labels these two sides "the traditional reading" and "the alternative reading" but acknowledges also that "[the Matthean writer's] main interest lies elsewhere." Lincoln, *Born of a Virgin?*, 95–98.

10. See also Nolland, "No Son-of-God Christology," 3–12.

of a miraculous conception assists us in explaining the outcome of the story in verse 25 because Joseph is there as the husband of Mary naming the born son in a parental role. We might think that identifying the child's biological origins explains why Joseph can easily step into a paternal role, namely Joseph is able to be there because the child has no other human father. In other words, if the child is conceived miraculously (nonsexually) this paves the way for Joseph by giving him the paternal role.

However, miraculous conception does not clarify such an outcome from Joseph's perspective. Even if Joseph had imagined in verse 18 that Mary's pregnancy "was *produced by* the Holy Spirit," that is not enough to clarify to Joseph what his role should now be. Even if Joseph were to be expressly told that Mary is having God's baby, such information alone does not clarify what Joseph is to do. It would still not be clear to Joseph whether such knowledge is welcoming him into the picture or pushing him aside. In order for Joseph to decide what he should be doing, Joseph requires clarification of his role since, from Joseph's perspective, merely knowing either that Mary is carrying another man's child or carrying God's own child is not enough to clarify his role in the situation.

What clarifies Joseph's role is when Joseph is given an instruction about what to do, namely when the angel tells Joseph to be the husband of Mary and take Mary his wife in verse 20. Then, when the angel tells Joseph that he should give the child a particular name this further clarifies Joseph's role. The marital role is clarified with an instruction and the parental role is clarified with a prediction/instruction. Although it may seem to us as if the idea of a miraculous, nonhuman conception explains the outcome, it is not necessarily the idea itself but only when it is combined with the two instructions given to Joseph concerning the clarification of his marital role and parental role.

The fact that conception is omitted leaves what previously happened (for Mary to already be pregnant) as a mystery. In theory, the option for imagining how Mary's holy child might have been conceived remains possible to imagine for those who choose to go there in order to try to get to the story that the writer is not telling. It is no wonder that Christian audiences of Matthew soon combined the story with Luke and took Matt 1:18–20 to be about Mary's virginal conception. At the same time, others took the silence as an admission that Mary's pregnancy must be the result of rape (perhaps by a Roman soldier). Any hypothesis looking to specify biological conception remains hypothetical. The verses in Matthew do not adequately function to justify a single theory of conception.

The issue is also affected by how we might think of the earlier references to heirs "produced" beginning with Abraham in verse 2. If we think that "Abraham produced Isaac" is a reference to the biological/sexual moment of "procreating" then we might also be likely to expect to be reading about biological conception in Matt 1:18–25. But the earlier references to patriarchs bringing forth heirs are more likely to be referencing the larger process of heir acquisition (legal inheritance). Similarly, the story in verses 18–25 is about how Jesus ended up becoming known as the son of Joseph, son of David (how Joseph acquired Jesus in his lineage) and not about how Mary conceived.

The idea of a "missing" conception reveals our own expectations of what we think the story should be saying. Why conception was not considered necessary for the story to tell can only be determined according to what *is* considered necessary according to the story itself.

In conclusion, miraculous conception is not given the kind of prominence within the story that is usually assumed. In fact, the Messiah's progeneration is not based on his biological conception which is probably why it skips over the conception and instead emphasizes the relationship of Joseph with Mary and of Joseph with Mary's child. The story speaks hopefully and theologically of the outcome, namely the significance of the child's characteristic nature and mission (to save his people from their sins) as later becomes evident in his life. The guarantor of Mary's pregnancy is God who endorses Mary's child as Joseph's heir and as a future savior clarifying Joseph's necessary marital role with Mary and parental role for the child. This amazing child is the appropriate heir for "Joseph son of David."

Scandalous rumors about Mary's pregnancy

Another popular assumption is that it has already occurred to some people within the story that Joseph is not the biological father and, consequently, scandalous rumors have begun to circulate about Mary.

Are any scandalous rumors expressly mentioned in the text? No.

Are scandalous rumors compatible with the text? No. The text gives insight into a story of which the public (within the story) was unaware. There is no clear evidence for any public knowledge that Mary is carrying a child that is already known to be someone else's child and not Joseph's child. In fact, in the first few verses, it is not even clear that anyone else (besides Mary and Joseph) knows that Mary is pregnant.

It will be helpful to examine the verb underlying "it was found" (εὑρέθη) in verse 18.

Greek-English Diglot (Matt 1:18)

Τοῦ δὲ Ἰησοῦ Χριστοῦ ἡ γένεσις οὕτως ἦν. μνηστευθείσης τῆς μητρὸς αὐτοῦ Μαρίας τῷ Ἰωσήφ, πρὶν ἢ συνελθεῖν αὐτοὺς εὑρέθη ἐν γαστρὶ ἔχουσα ἐκ πνεύματος ἁγίου. (SBLGNT)

The Jesus-Messiah's progeneration was this way. His mother Mary being betrothed to Joseph, before they united, it was found she had a belly from the Holy Spirit.

The verb "was found" (εὑρέθη) roughly connects back to Mary as subject. It also connects forward by introducing the following situation where it attaches to "in belly having from Holy Spirit" (ἐν γαστρὶ ἔχουσα ἐκ πνεύματος ἁγίου).[11] In other words, "they were not united yet already she was pregnant."

The sense "already" is not something additional to the text since here the sense of the verb (εὑρέθη) is that what became evident was already the case just before it was noticed. There is a similar use of the same verb in Luke 9:36 where it indicates that something was by then the case, namely "when the voice sounded/happened, Jesus was found alone" (καὶ ἐν τῷ γενέσθαι τὴν φωνὴν εὑρέθη Ἰησοῦς μόνος).

In Luke 9:36, the verb "was found" (εὑρέθη) is not a reference to the public "finding" Jesus or to a secret being revealed to the public. The people to whom it "was found" are simply the three disciples there who have been watching the event. What was "found" is simply the realization that Jesus is no longer accompanied by Moses and Elijah (apparently then "only Jesus was left" εὑρέθη Ἰησοῦς μόνος). In other words, εὑρέθη in this type of application expresses that something had eventuated and become evident to the immediate characters participating in the story.

Similarly, εὑρέθη in Matt 1:18 does not necessarily refer to any public "discovery" since it appears for the benefit of the story's audience and it would apply to the knowledge of the persons just mentioned (Mary and

11. The expected subject of the verb εὑρέθη is that it will not be Mary since "Mary his mother" is the previous subject of the genitive absolute ("being betrothed") suggesting that the next subject (of the main verb εὑρέθη) will be a subject separate from "Mary his mother." So "in belly her having from the Holy Spirit" could be taken to be the subject of the verb, as though Mary's "pregnant belly" is the subject of "was found to be."

Joseph). Something has already eventuated for Mary and Joseph, namely "pregnancy" (Mary is *already* pregnant).

For the sake of thinking through the idea of alleged public discovery more comprehensively, consider the following diagram for identifying to whom such knowledge occurred. If we are open to all possibilities, there are various possible referents for εὑρέθη.

Those for whom the knowledge of pregnancy is most obvious would be the text's audience who knows that Mary "has a pregnant belly." We could visualize the remaining options as outer "layers" of persons further removed but potentially possessing the same knowledge.

Figure 4. Inner circles of knowledge.

Moving beyond the obvious "knowers" (readers and hearers of the story), we could assume that Mary herself is included as having knowledge of her own pregnancy (in fact εὑρέθη could even mean "she realized").[12] Within this same orbit (or sphere of knowledge) we could hypothesize that

---

12. Schweizer, takes εὑρέθη to mean "she [Mary] found out that." Schweizer, *The Good News*, 26.

there are other possible members in the same household to which Mary belongs who might simultaneously know that Mary is pregnant.

The next logical layer of knowledge is Joseph. We could infer that Joseph is included in noticing that Mary is pregnant. In fact, the most relevant referents for the verb εὑρέθη within the story are the two people already mentioned in the story, in this case Mary *and Joseph*. Furthermore, the next verse immediately focuses on Joseph as though he was included in the "realization" of εὑρέθη.

It is doubtful that we are expected to stretch verse 18 to say that Mary's pregnancy is also *public* knowledge. The next verse focuses on Joseph's planned response as though the issue is about what the public will soon *potentially* know, depending on Joseph. Joseph's decision will affect what the public will know. Apparently, the public is on the brink of seeing/knowing that Mary and Joseph are having a child. It will soon become apparent to others. Joseph is deciding what that public knowledge will or will not look like.

If verse 18 is not saying that the public have noticed that Mary is pregnant then it is also not saying that the public would think she is pregnant to someone other than Joseph.

There are four potential assertions we might make: (1) the public does not yet know about Mary's pregnancy; (2) the public only knows that Mary is pregnant; (3) it has become public knowledge that Mary is pregnant but no rumors have yet begun to spread about Mary; or (4) the public knows that Joseph is not the father of Mary's pregnancy and rumors are starting to spread.

The first assertion (the public knows nothing yet) seems most reasonable to suppose according to verse 18 but it pays also to consider how we read πρὶν ἤ συνελθεῖν ("before they became united") because this affects how much public knowledge we are willing to import into the story. Whether we take πρὶν ἤ συνελθεῖν as a reference to Mary and Joseph's not yet "living together" or to their not yet "having sexual intercourse" the implication is that we (the audience) are being told that no sexual union between Mary and Joseph has occurred.

This is not a publicly "known" detail. If we were to look for all the publicly known details expressly mentioned within verses 18–25 we will see that no publicly known details appear until the story's conclusion when Joseph "took" Mary and then Mary "gave birth" and the child is "named." Only in the outcome of the story are publicly known details mentioned. Even within this publicly knowable outcome, it mentions again that Joseph has not had sex with Mary (v. 25) without any implication that this is something publicly known ("he did not have sexual relations with her prior to the time she gave birth to a son" καὶ οὐκ ἐγίνωσκεν αὐτὴν ἕως οὗ ἔτεκεν υἱόν).

There is no reason to assume that this reference to lack of sexual intercourse is common knowledge. It seems reasonable to apply the same logic to the first reference in verse 18 as to the second reference in verse 25. Both times that no sexual union is mentioned it is providing an insight that is not something known by the public who are implied to exist within the story.

If verse 18 is not saying what the public knew of Mary's pregnancy, then it is also not saying that other people knew that Joseph was not the father. No one else would know this unless Mary and Joseph have said something about the paternity. The text does not support the idea that either Mary or Joseph has told other people that Joseph is not the father. In fact, Joseph is expressly presented as *not* willing to say anything about what he knows in verse 19.

Verse 19 will be explained in much more detail in the following chapter. For now, it is enough to point out that Joseph's planned response demonstrates his intentions are to avoid going public with what he knows (so as not to disgrace Mary) and he intends not to be married to Mary (he intends to dissolve the marriage arrangement privately). Both references to Joseph's intentions are nonpublic as though Joseph does not want the public to know the details of their sexual relationship (or lack thereof).

One problem with supposing sex details being "publicly known" is that it makes verse 19 about Joseph *responding* to public reaction rather than *anticipating* public reaction and such a position is difficult to sustain according to the text. Why would it suddenly seem like Joseph really is the father at the end of the story vignette as though scandalous rumors suddenly disappear? It is as if rumors were never an issue in the first place.

To assume scandalous rumors within the story would be to spoil the tension between public and private perspectives, namely the perspective the public have of what it looks like from the outside and the private perspective that Mary and Joseph (and God and the text's audience) share in knowing about the situation.

In conclusion, whether or not Mary has had sex is not something that the text is claiming to be publicly known or knowable. According to the story vignette, what was publicly known is simply that Mary gave birth after having been apparently pregnant with Joseph's child—there being no reason to suspect anything unusual from the perspective of the public. According to verse 19, Joseph is anticipating avoiding certain knowledge becoming public. In other words, there is the *potential* for public knowledge if Joseph were to say something

Why might someone hold the assumption of public rumors? Someone might infer a public scandal if they suppose that other people knew that it was not Joseph's child. The idea of scandalous rumors might seem appealing because of the potential to see Mary and Joseph courageously battling through public scandal (after Joseph is told to marry Mary by the angel). That might be an interesting story to us, but it is not the story according to Matthew 1. Of course, there is the potential for scandal if Joseph were to say something but no scandal ever eventuates because Joseph is not willing to allow what he knows to become public.

Forbidden "premarital" sex

An alternate assumption to the previous one is an assumption that the public thought that Mary was carrying Joseph's child and people were shocked that Mary and Joseph have apparently not waited until the wedding night to begin sexual relations. In other words, Mary and Joseph were supposed to be abstaining from sex but by not abstaining they were considered to have committed "fornication." This assumption faces the same challenges as the previous assumption. But it is worthwhile considering its specific flaws.

Is forbidden premarital sex mentioned in the text? No, the text does not mention that Mary and Joseph were thought by the public to be forbidden to have sex with each other.

Is forbidden premarital sex compatible with the story? No. Firstly, planning a quiet divorce would not solve anything if the problem really was a rumor about shameful/forbidden premarital sex.

Secondly, even if we were to entertain the notion that Mary's pregnancy is considered public knowledge in verse 18, the notion of forbidden sex is incompatible with the story. According to the way marriages are assumed to work in biblical texts, a betrothed couple having "premarital" sex is not considered "fornication" because fornication (*porneia*) is when a couple have sex who are *ineligible* to be considered a couple.

Without any known legal impediments for a couple like Mary and Joseph being considered "together" their union is not "forbidden" in the way that certain couplings were considered forbidden (such as being too closely related, or being not closely enough related). If Mary is thought to be eligible to Joseph then she is not forbidden to be carrying Joseph's child.

If it looks like Mary and Joseph are having a child together and they are not ineligible to marry then it is not an example of fornication as the couple would appear married. The idea of legality does not derive from a government certificate but from their families' opinion and from public opinion.

How marriages are formalized in the stories of Abraham, Isaac, and Jacob can be compared to how a marriage is formalized in the book of Tobit. In both, it is the families' opinion that formalizes the union. In the book of Tobit, the process for Tobiah and Sarah proceeds without a betrothal period. Eligibility is determined (Tob 6:12–13; 7:9–11); the woman is given to the man with a verbal declaration (Tob 7:11–12); the agreement is put in writing (Tob 7:13); they eat and drink (Tob 7:14); then the bride and groom sleep together that night (Tob 7:15–16; 8:4–9). In Tobit, this all happens in a single day; there is no need for a period of betrothal prior to the marriage.

The mention of a betrothal in Matthew 1 would remind readers and hearers of the marriages mentioned for the patriarchs from the book of Genesis, especially since the idea of having a betrothal period was only revived *after* the book of Matthew was published.[13] It is intriguing that in the case of Mary and Joseph, Mary is betrothed to Joseph as though Joseph were like the patriarchs of old planning ahead to formalize bonds between the two families. The concept of betrothal highlights the theme of patriarchal intentions (a theme continued in verse 19).

Another question to answer is why Joseph would think that to dissolve the betrothal he would need to divorce Mary. Some scholars look to later rabbinic law for the answer (where dissolving unwanted betrothals would require a certificate of divorce).[14] But we can find the answer within the text of Matthew 1. If Joseph is anticipating what will soon become the public

13. Satlow argues, "Our extant evidence suggests that this legal structure of marriage—consisting of a first stage of 'betrothal' followed (perhaps some significant period of time later) by consummation and cohabitation—simply did not continue among Jews from the biblical period onwards. With only one exception [Matt 1:18–19], both literary sources and legal documents found on papyri written from the sixth century BCE to the first century CE suggest that Jews did not 'betroth' in this manner." Even for the later rabbis, when betrothal periods were being revived, there was "a rabbinic debate about whether sex alone (with or without a statement of intention) can cause a couple to marry." Satlow, "A Detached Kiddushin."

14. Zaas, "Matthew's Birth Story," 125–28.

opinion (v. 19), he will need to make it legal for Mary to (re)marry otherwise everyone will soon think that Mary is Joseph's pregnant wife.

In other words, if Joseph is planning to dissolve the relationship without revealing that his marriage remains unconsummated it will mean that divorce is necessary. He would need to make it clear that Mary is not his wife, otherwise he would need to tell people that he has not yet had sexual relations with Mary. But that would be to say something to shame Mary (which contradicts verse 19). If he does not intend to appear married and if he does not intend to say something to shame Mary, how else is Mary to be free to remarry unless she is no longer known as Joseph's wife? Legally, Mary should be free to be married to whoever's child she is having. Whoever's child it is should be able to be known as the father so the child can know, and be known by, the appropriate paternity.

Why might someone assume that the public thought Mary and Joseph were forbidden to have sex? The idea of "forbidden premarital sex" may be appealing to modern Christian audiences wishing to impose later Christian assumptions about premarital sex onto the story to make the story seem more relevant.

Also, someone might hold this assumption because it might seem to explain how the story vignette concludes in verses 24–25. Perhaps Joseph stays with Mary without going public about his nonpaternity which hastens the wedding date so that Mary's child can be born several months after the wedding. However, no wedding details appear in the story. The story is not about a wedding. It is about introducing us to an insight that the public never had, namely Joseph's initial nonpaternity of Mary's child and unconsummated marriage with Mary. Joseph, though not being the biological father of Mary's child, somehow becomes publicly known as the father. The story tells how that eventuated.

Expected execution: Joseph should have handed Mary over to be executed

Another popular assumption is that Joseph was expected to take Mary to court to be put on trial and sentenced to death if he thought Mary had committed adultery.

Is execution mentioned in the text? No. Execution is not mentioned in the text (not according to the Greek text of Matthew, but see below, concerning Hebrew manuscripts).

Is execution compatible with the text? No. Expected execution is not quite compatible with the text for numerous reasons.

Firstly, the execution "laws" in Deuteronomy were not the laws of the land under Roman rule. Under Roman rule, if a local Jewish court believed that execution was necessary it would need to hand the matter over to the Roman authorities, as seen later in Matthew when Jesus is handed over to the Roman authorities for execution.[15]

Secondly, Joseph's situation is unlike the kind of situations depicted in Deut 22:13–27 dealing with a variety of hypothetical cases, some of which concern adultery. But in every case of execution the situation is already public. The public have already caught the man and woman together (or the public already have confessions). Basically, the public knows what has happened because it has come to public attention. This is very different to what we find in Joseph's case in Matt 1:18 in which no man has been witnessed with Mary and there is yet no public discussion of any issue.

If Joseph were to go public with what he knows (that he is not the father because he has not had sex with Mary) then Joseph's case could turn out to be like the first hypothetical case of the slanderous husband (Deut 22:13–21). The slanderous husband went public but he should not have done so. He is portrayed as being unhappy with his new bride and so he went about slandering her, saying that he didn't think she was a virgin after all. The text is showing that the slanderous husband should not have done that because that was a wrong way of addressing his concerns. By not going public, Joseph is not like the slanderous husband.

In fact, Joseph, as a solitary witness, is not expected to bring accusations against Mary unless it has already become public knowledge or unless there are already other witnesses. Unless there are multiple witnesses to the crime then a solitary witness is not allowed to try to begin such a trial, according to biblical law, otherwise it would be an illegitimate trial (see Num 35:30b; Deut 17:6; 19:15) and would be merely one person's word against another person's word resulting in Mary's being defamed and unjustly shamed.

---

15. The story depicted in John 8 cannot be taken as evidence that Jewish courts in Jerusalem were executing adulterers in the first century. John 8 does not depict a court scene since the local elders of the community are not present and the man allegedly caught with the woman is also not there. Also, when Jesus is later handed over to Pilate it is acknowledged that "it is not permitted for us to execute anyone" (John 18:31b). So John 8 is depicting a trap question similar to the question of whether or not the people should pay taxes to Caesar in Matt 22:15–22.

Another reason that execution is not the expected outcome is that if we look at the variety of biblical references to what outcome people usually expected when adultery had occurred, we find that the expected outcome was not execution by a court (see Prov 6:32–38; 18:22 in which it is expected that there is no trial and that the husband will take matters into his own hands). In Jer 3:8 the outcome for dealing with the "adultery" is with a certificate of divorce. Num 5:11–31 details a hypothetical case for a suspicious husband, who is very jealous of his wife and wants to take her back as his own wife but he thinks that she has committed adultery. Since she has not been caught he does not have evidence but he does not know if he can still have her as his wife. So the text advises a sort of private trial that he could put her on. If she *is* declared guilty of adultery by the trial she is *not* executed.

By comparison, Joseph is not like the desperately jealous husband in Num 5:11–31 overcome with a spirit of jealousy and wanting to be able to take his wife back but who cannot. Joseph, by contrast, has not even taken Mary yet and he is not overcome with a spirit of jealousy. Instead he is willing to let Mary go.

Furthermore, according to what we find later in Matthew, the expected outcome for adultery is divorce, based largely on the way that Deut 24:1–4 came to be understood as being about adultery and divorce. Deuteronomy 24 concerns a husband not being allowed to remarry his wife after divorce (if people knew she was clearly divorced from him with a certificate of divorce, after he found something shameful about her, and she marries somebody else and the second husband also divorces her then the first husband cannot take her again as his wife).

According to Matt 5:31–32 and Matt 19:9, Jesus is quoted as saying that whenever a man divorces his wife thinking he can marry another woman it is not a valid divorce from the first wife unless it is already a case of *porneia* ("unlawful union" or "fornication"). This assumes that adultery was the expected outcome for cases of *porneia*. In Matthew, divorce was apparently the expected outcome in cases of adultery and suspected adultery.

In all, according to biblical ethics and according to Matthew, Joseph is not expected to be bringing accusations against Mary by starting a trial for her to be executed.

Why might someone assume that execution is the expected outcome? The primary reason why someone might import the notion of execution into the text is based on a willingness to speculate that the expected "story conflict" that emerges is not something mentioned in the text.

Another reason for the assumption is based on an alternative way of reading what it says about Joseph "not wanting to shame her" (v. 19). Rather than reading it as "Joseph, her husband, being righteous" as the logical *reason* for him not wanting to disgrace Mary, it is possible to read it concessively as an accommodation or compromise, as saying, "Joseph, her husband, *though being* righteous, he did not want to shame her."

Such a reading, oddly, assumes that Joseph shaming Mary would make him righteous as though Jewish law would require it. There are several problems with this interpretation (as already noted) including the odd idea that righteousness requires exposing someone to public shame—an idea that seems at odds with biblical ethics. Also, handing Mary over for execution is not expected practice. The idea seems to reflect a later Christian bias incompatible with the text since if Joseph is seen to be righteous by *resisting* expected execution it makes Joseph seem like he is better than the Jewish practices of his day, which seems to be an assumption that does not fit the kind of assumptions elsewhere in Matthew in which it is considered a good thing to be obeying biblical commandments (Matt 5:17–19) and a good thing to heed what is taught by the scribes and Pharisees (Matt 23:3).

So it seems to be unnecessary to suppose an expectation of execution in the first place. Without the assumption of execution, there is little reason to take Joseph's "being righteous" concessively/resistantly (as "though being righteous").[16]

Having said that, there is an alternate Hebrew version of Matthew attested from the fourteenth century (also known as "Shem Tob's Hebrew Matthew") and it includes two extra clauses in verse 19, one of which indicates an expectation of execution:

Hebrew-English Diglot (Matt 1:19)

ויוסף איש צדיק היה ולא רצה לישב עמה	Joseph was a righteous man. He did
ולא לגלותה להביאה לבושה	not want to live with her, or to call her
ולא לאוסרה למות אבל היה רוצה לכסות עליה.	out, or to hand her over for death. He wanted to keep her secret.[17]

16. It is not entirely incorrect to see a tension between Joseph and something else in the story since Joseph seems to be presented as being different from *something*. That something is explored in the following chapter.

17. The translation is mine; the Hebrew is from Howard, *Hebrew Gospel of Matthew*, 4.

The Hebrew here looks like an expanded version of verse 19 from our Greek Matthew. Joseph's intentions are now further clarified in four clauses rather than two. Here, the potential for execution is mentioned ("nor to hand her over for death" ולא לאוסרה למות). Is this evidence that mention of execution is a further explanation for what "bring her to shame" meant in Greek Matthew? Or is "hand her over to death" given distinctly as another thing that Joseph is not willing to do?

While I will not be examining Hebrew Matt 1:18–25 here—it would require its own focused investigation—my initial assessment is that this portion of Hebrew Matthew appears to reflect a later Christian missionary interpretation. In order for execution to be an expected option for Joseph, the text of Hebrew Matthew supposes that execution for adultery was being practiced at the time. Such an assumption seems to be, predominantly, a later Christian interpretation of Jewish history.

By contrast, Jewish commentaries on Greek Matthew do not tend to include an assumption of expected execution when interpreting the Greek text of Matthew.[18] This is usually because Jewish commentators tend to suppose that execution for adultery was not mandated by biblical law nor was it practiced during the Roman period. Jewish commentators tend to assume divorce to be the expected outcome in cases of adultery and suspected adultery—an assumption which fits better with what seems to be assumed elsewhere in the book of Matthew.

Some readers may be willing (or eager) to speculate on reconstructing the historical situation concerning the "historical Mary" and "historical Joseph" to which the story seems to be referring. The idea of execution might seem to be adding compatible information in order to make sense of Joseph's decision. This may seem especially appealing if Joseph's decision is not clearly explained within the story or if it is difficult to follow the logic of verse 19.

In all, the assumption is not very compatible with the Greek text. It will become clear in the following chapter that the text makes good sense without the assumption of execution.

18. Levine, "Matthew," 341. Lachs, *A Rabbinic Commentary*, 6. Soloveitchik, *The Bible the Talmud*, 68. Basser, *The Mind Behind the Gospels*, 32, allows for a death penalty in theory if a number of conditions were met in order that strong proof be provided.

Joseph wrongly assumed Mary was guilty of adultery

The fifth assumption to address is that Joseph simply assumed that Mary was guilty of adultery which is why he (wrongly) intended to divorce her.

Is adultery mentioned in the story? No. The reason for Joseph's plan to divorce is not mentioned, so the assumption needs to be unpacked by considering why we think we would be able to guess what Joseph was thinking and to articulate the evidence within the text for this assumption.

How compatible is adultery with Matt 1:18–25? The assumption is complex. The three main components of the assumption are:

1. Joseph knows that the child Mary is carrying is not his child so he is presumably feeling betrayed by Mary;

2. Joseph's plan to divorce shows he did not want to be married to someone he assumes to be an adulterous woman; and

3. Joseph is told that his plan to divorce Mary is wrong as though his plan was based on a wrong assumption and so the angel is rebuking Joseph and defending Mary's innocence.

When we examine each component of the assumption, only one aspect is compatible with the text, that is, the idea of an adulterous union is relevant in some way but the evidence points in a different direction than to Mary's past.

The first component contains two elements: (a) Joseph knows that the child is not his and (b) he feels betrayed. The second element lacks any evidence in the text. Joseph would be correctly assuming (a) that the child is not his. But nowhere in the text is Joseph portrayed as feeling betrayed by Mary. We might assume that Joseph feels betrayed by his "woman" (the word we translate as "wife" is simply the word "woman") given that Mary was originally meant to be his woman and the child she was meant to be having was originally meant to be Joseph's child. That was the plan but now that plan is ruined if Mary is now having someone else's child. In theory, we might imagine Joseph being resentful of Mary by seeing her as the one to blame. He might be feeling cheated on by Mary and/or feeling jealous.

However, there is nothing in the text presenting Joseph as feeling hurt, betrayed, jealous, or resentful. The only emotion indicated in the story is his fear to be married. The portrait of Joseph appearing in verses 18–25 is of a man fearfully stepping aside. Any feelings of jealousy or betrayal are our own importations we might assume on behalf of the man we think Joseph was rather than the Joseph presented in the text.

It is helpful to consider the two Greek terms used for unlawful unions in Matthew: "adultery" (μοιχεία) and the more general term usually translated as "fornication" (πορνεία). The latter term, *porneia*, refers to any unsanctioned sexual union while *moicheia* is the creation of an unsanctioned sexual union by breaking an already existing union, namely marriage (so μοιχεία could be considered a specific type of πορνεία). For example, in Matt 5:32 Jesus is quoted as teaching his disciples that for men who divorce their wives it is only valid in cases of already existing *porneia* otherwise the man divorcing his wife turns the next marriage into a case of adultery by breaking an existing (sanctioned) union with a new (unlawful) union. According to this logic, unless a union is already invalid (characterized by *porneia*), another marriage creates an invalid union (adultery).

It is also helpful to consider the story of the first Joseph in the book of Genesis. In Genesis 39, Potiphar's wife is portrayed as requesting Joseph to "lay" with her illicitly and Joseph resists, saying that he could never do such a "bad sinful thing" (he does not use the term for an unlawful sexual union/adultery). Later, Potiphar's wife effectively accuses Joseph of attempted rape so that Joseph is thrown into prison. So the first Joseph managed to avoid being guilty of an illicit union but nevertheless ended up being imprisoned anyway.

The reason the first Joseph became known as Joseph "the righteous" was because he was not willing to illicitly have sex with Potiphar's wife.[19] It does not seem to be a coincidence that the second Joseph is also identified as "righteous" because of his unwillingness to take Mary unjustly. It would seem that both Josephs are resisting some kind of unlawful/adulterous relationship.

A parallel between the first and second Josephs is strengthened by the fact of the resemblance of the two Josephs having the same birth name (both are "Joseph, son of Jacob"); both have a common intention (to avoid *porneia*); and both consequently are known for being "righteous." It seems likely that early audiences of Matthew 1 would immediately recognize the same theme of *Joseph resisting an unlawful union* in which the second Joseph lives up to his namesake.

---

19. Loader concludes, "Joseph [from Genesis] was seen as a model of resisting adultery (Wis 10:13; 4 Macc 2:2–3; Philo Ios 40–44; Josephus *A.J.* 2.41–60)." Loader, *New Testament on Sexuality*, 5.

However, the idea of resisting *porneia* is the only part of the assumption compatible with Matt 1:18–25. Every other part of the assumption fails upon examination. It will be wise to consider the remaining parts of the assumption and to consider why there is no evidence in the text for them.

The second component of the assumption to examine is the idea that Joseph's plan to divorce shows he does not want Mary since he wrongly assumes her to be an adulterous woman. Although Joseph's plan to divorce seems to be indicating his aversion to some kind of *porneia*, it is not necessarily because Joseph thinks *Mary* is to blame.

Notice that it does not say "Joseph did not want to marry Mary and he decided not to shame her." Apparently, it is that he did not want to shame her (to disclose the situation) and so he decided to step aside (as nonpublicly as possible). But it is not necessarily saying that Joseph thought Mary would not make a good wife. In the story, there is no mention of personal aversion to Mary as being guilty or unworthy of Joseph.

One problem with this complex assumption is that we assume Joseph is making a wrong assumption about the situation or that he is actively refusing to listen to what Mary might have to say. So Joseph does not go to Mary and ask her to explain herself either because he is so sure that she has no excuse for cheating on him, or Joseph seems to be making a decision without talking to Mary as a sign that he is not interested in listening to her side of the story. The idea that Joseph is not making any attempt to find out whose child Mary is carrying can end up making Joseph seem quite arrogant and self-righteous.

However, that is not how Joseph is presented. The text presents Joseph's behavior favorably. Ian Boxall correctly points out that the ideal reader is expected "to applaud Joseph's good intentions."[20] When the text mentions that Joseph is "a righteous man" it presumably means someone who is inclined to do what is right and avoid what is wrong. But how can the right thing be not to ask any questions about Mary's pregnancy and simply make a wrong assumption? In order for a righteous person to correctly assess the right thing to do (or to avoid doing the wrong thing) it requires checking out the facts. Otherwise, Joseph is portrayed as someone who is acting wrongly by making a poor decision without even checking anything out or portrayed as someone unwilling to listen to anything Mary might have to say about her own pregnancy.

---

20. Boxall, *Discovering Matthew*, 84.

Yet Joseph is not presented as making wrong assumptions about Mary. Reading that idea into the story creates difficulties for the story by suggesting a kind of Joseph who is not so righteous after all. The story presents Joseph as not wanting to make things worse for Mary. If we think Joseph is getting things wrong, we are having difficulties understanding the logic in the text (the following chapter will unpack this logic).

The third and final component of the assumption to examine is that Joseph is told that his plan to divorce Mary is wrong which means his plan was based on a wrong assumption since the angel rebukes Joseph and defends Mary's innocence.

Does the angel rebuke Joseph? Without such an assumption driving our reading it seems instead that the angel's instruction ("Do not be afraid to take Mary your wife") is not an admonishment but an encouragement. The angel declares Joseph to be Mary's husband (or Mary to be Joseph's wife) because Joseph was afraid to take Mary given that she was not yet in a sexual relationship with him and she was having a child who was not his child. It would seem that Joseph is not being rebuked because he is not considered to be responding wrongly in the first place.

Note also that the angel does not seem to be defending Mary. Mary's past is not brought up (Mary is not the subject of the sentence in verse 20; Mary's child, the heir, is the subject). Many of us tend to read it as though Mary were being declared innocent of adultery against Joseph's wrong assumption. Rather, the text provides a declaration of how important the child is in terms of the child's destiny (as Joseph's heir within a Davidic lineage). The angel is talking about the child rather than Mary.

Notice also that Joseph does not seem to be very sorry. If his attitude toward Mary is blame (and is wrong) then why has his attitude not shifted? Should it not have mentioned that Joseph apologized to Mary for assuming the wrong thing about her or at least indicated that Joseph was sorry for not listening to her? Instead, it is Joseph's actions that are presented as shifting, not his attitude. It says, Joseph "got up and he did what he was told to do by the angel of the Lord." Joseph is not presented as being sorry because it is not his attitude (of blame) that is presented as changing.

The flaws in the assumption that, from Joseph's perspective, Mary is to blame for adultery should be taken as a sign that we are misreading the presentation of Joseph and seeing him as a self-righteous man, who got it wrong. The idea that Joseph feels Mary is to blame so that he is unwilling even to check anything with her seems incompatible with the way Joseph is presented. Perhaps Joseph is not being presented as judgmental or arrogant or needing to be rebuked by the angel. Perhaps Mary does not need to be defended against Joseph's wrong assumption. Perhaps such things are not in the text.

Finally, it tends to be assumed that because Joseph is told by an angel to follow a different plan then Joseph's intended plan must have been wrong. This is an unnecessary assumption. A new plan does not necessarily imply that an earlier plan was bad or wrong. The new plan might simply be a better plan from God, indicating an even greater goal with greater good.

The way most of us read verses 18–25 has been driven by an assumption of Joseph thinking the wrong thing about Mary's behavior and planning to do the wrong thing even though it hardly seems very compatible with the text.

Why would someone hold to the assumption that the story is about Joseph misjudging Mary? There are three overlapping reasons.

Firstly, many of us do not know any other way of reading the story. We simply read it that way because we have been taught to read it that way. Most modern commentaries do not introduce any viable alternatives nor do they mention the flaws in this very popular assumption.

Secondly, we tend to read what Joseph is planning to do as being "wrong" because we know that is not the "correct" outcome of what will eventuate. We know that in the end Joseph and Mary will be husband and wife and the child will be raised as Joseph's heir. So we imagine that what Joseph was planning to do must be wrong because Joseph is given a different plan to follow.

Thirdly, we need an explanation as to why Joseph is about to do the "wrong" thing by divorcing Mary. The popular assumption fills this need by suggesting that Joseph's plan is wrong because he wrongly assumed that Mary had committed adultery.

In all, unpacking the whole assumption reveals it to be an excellent example of how the text has been read according to an assumption rather than checking the assumption according to the text. What is really going on with Joseph and what he was thinking remains to be unpacked in the following chapter.

Critical assessment of the five assumptions

The preceding five popular assumptions reveal that much of what passes as the story in Matt 1:18–25 is an unnecessary imposition. These ideas may be obscuring the story in the text by distracting us with imposed interpretations.

Although the idea of Mary conceiving Jesus asexually is potentially an empowering notion, Mary's conception of Jesus is not prominent in the story nor even mentioned in the story. Modern influences of biology and history seem to have significantly shaped our perception of reading and distorted how we read the entire story vignette according to the imposed idea of conception.

Back in the fourth century, John Chrysostom accepted the idea that Mary became pregnant miraculously from the Holy Spirit (partly because he willingly combined the story in Matthew with Luke). Yet even Chrysostom thought it unwise, indeed offensive, to go "beyond the text" by enquiring as to how Mary became pregnant:

> Do not speculate beyond the text. Do not require of it something more than what it simply says . . . Shame on those who attempt to pry into the miracle of generation from on high! . . . What kind of extreme madness afflicts those who busy themselves by curiously prying into the unutterable generation?[21]

Chrysostom's reason for not going beyond the text is that it would be disrespectful as we are simply not given the right to such knowledge. The same logic might be applied to Mary, namely we might also respect the lack of mention of how Mary conceived since assuming a miraculous conception is not the only way for readers and hearers to be respectful toward Mary. According to the text, it is apparently sufficient to focus on the child's future and so Mary's conception is omitted and therefore remains mysterious.

Note that all five imported ideas (conception; scandalous rumors; forbidden premarital sex; expected execution; and Joseph's wrong assessment of Mary's alleged adultery) make the story vignette about Mary's sexuality as though what was going on with Mary's body is key to the story. This is perhaps easiest to notice with the first assumption (conception) in which commentators tend to overestimate the importance of knowing something of the biological process of Mary conceiving her child.

21. Chrysostom, "The Gospel of Matthew," 12.

The second assumption (scandalous rumors) overestimated what people might have been thinking and saying about Mary as though the story were about Mary already being publicly disgraced despite what verse 19 says.

Similarly, the third assumption presumed that people were talking about Mary having forbidden premarital sex with Joseph which, again, is incompatible with verse 19.

The fourth assumption (expected execution) overestimated knowledge of the legal practice of execution for women caught in adultery or even suspected of adultery in order to read the text within such a presumed hyper-judgmental context of women's bodies, something incompatible with the Matthean text.

The fifth assumption overestimated the negative thoughts and feelings that Joseph was allegedly thinking and feeling about Mary, namely that he was disgusted and/or feeling betrayed by Mary's presumed unfaithfulness.

These popular assumptions tell us more about ourselves and our own way of reading than about the text. All five assumptions overestimate the importance of the idea of monitoring Mary's body. Not only do these misassumptions tell us about the willingness of commentators to have the story vignette controlled by things not in the text, they also tell us about the commentator's own perception that the story concerns the control of Mary's body thereby revealing patriarchal tendencies at work in front of the text. The idea that the story is asking us to focus on Mary's body or about what Joseph thinks Mary has done sexually is not encouraged by the text. In fact, the idea that Mary's sexual fidelity is being assessed by anyone in the story is forestalled in the story itself. Why then have so many Matthean commentators reinstated it? The story, according to the text, focuses on other issues such as the child's future, Joseph's intentions, Joseph's relationships and Joseph's actions.

In other words, the story as it is usually told to Christians, with the usual above assumptions, seems suspiciously like the kind of patriarchal thinking within the commentator's own world—assessing the woman and (mis)judging what she is doing or has done within a virgin-whore binary (condemning the whore; praising the virgin). No wonder feminist and womanist interpreters resist such readings.[22] Sometimes, as it turns out in Matthew 1, such interpretations are not promoted by the text but by the mind (or world) of the commentator.

22. For one example, see Smith, "Fashioning Our Own Souls," 158–82.

Whatever the patriarchal message in the story might be, it is not of the same kind of patriarchy that has been assumed within the popular commentary tradition. For many of us, assumptions have been made about Mary's sexuality and the perception of her conception of her child. Yet, according to what is written, the audience of Matthew is not encouraged to speculate on such things.

Having now assessed the popular reading assumptions and found what is *not* there, we can begin now to look more closely at what *is* there.

5

How Joseph is Right: The Poetics of Joseph's Necessary Plan in Matt 1:19

Overview

This chapter looks at what Joseph was thinking in verse 19 where he is avoiding publicly claiming Mary as his wife as well as avoiding publicly disclaiming Mary. Joseph is presented as an atypical man by behaving unexpectedly which is why it labels him a "righteous" man. The same use of the label is found later in Matthew. In the two later cases in Matthew in which a known character is identified as "righteous" (Abel and Jesus) as well in the two earlier scriptural examples (Noah and Job) the label is (δίκαιος/צדיק) meaning "inculpable" or "innocent" suggesting "a man unlike other men." Such a man is not inclined to be doing what other men do. Other men in Joseph's situation would either have been inclined to say what they knew about their own nonpaternity (and thereby end up disgracing Mary) or they would have self-servingly claimed Mary and her child for themselves. Neither option is considered right for Joseph, hence it was initially right for Joseph not to claim Mary and her child and it was right for Joseph to claim Mary and her child when divinely sanctioned.

JOSEPH'S INITIAL PLAN TO divorce Mary might seem to be an unnecessary diversion. It could have simply said something like, "Mary was already pregnant, from the Holy Spirit, when she was betrothed to Joseph but Joseph was commanded to take Mary as his wife by an angel of the Lord. All this occurred so that what was spoken by the Lord through the prophet would be fulfilled" (followed by verses 23 to 25). If the purpose of the story was to show Joseph's obedience to an angel's instruction, it seems unnecessary to mention that Joseph initially planned to divorce

67

Mary. This leaves us with an important text-based question: If Joseph's plan seems so unnecessary to mention from our perspective then why was it so necessary for this very short story to include it?

The usual reasons given in the commentaries are not very compatible with the text. If Joseph really is being depicted as a man making wrong assumptions about Mary's past and is apparently uninterested in hearing what Mary had to say about her own pregnancy (and making wrong plans) then why is he called righteous? Something does not add up.

It is sometimes said that verses 18–25 present Joseph's perspective. Yet the story presents a perspective greater than Joseph's. It is not until verse 20 that we would say that we see or hear what Joseph sees or hears. Is the audience expected to be able to guess what Joseph was thinking prior to verse 20? The distance between our perspective and whatever we might guess is Joseph's initial perspective (vv. 18–19) makes it difficult for us to empathize with Joseph's more limited perspective.[1]

Joseph's presence in verses 18–19 quickly establishes him as the main character in this episode who participates in the majority of the verbs (in Matt 1:18–25, Joseph is the subject of fifty percent of the verbs; compare Mary at fifteen per cent; God at fifteen per cent; Jesus at ten per cent).

The most commonly repeated element is Joseph's relationship to Mary which is mentioned seven times in verses 18–25.[2] According to the story, Joseph and Mary ultimately being together is very important. Joseph is depicted as initially resisting being known as Mary's husband. Why? The short answer is that verses 18 and 19 are about *potential* outcomes being at odds with the *eventual* outcome. In other words, Joseph is only able to reach the eventual outcome with divine intervention so the story emphasizes the necessary divine assistance.

Why Joseph's divorce plan seems at odds with the expected outcome is because the story does not begin with Joseph's knowledge of what to do and because we (unlike Joseph) already know how the story ends before it begins. If we were to stop reading at the end of verse 18 and ask what the outcome of the story will be we can answer this even if we have never read any further than verse 18 because we already know the story's eventual

---

1. Yamasaki explains the importance of creating empathy with a character. See Yamasaki, *Perspective Criticism*.

2. μνηστευθείσης τῆς μητρὸς αὐτοῦ Μαρίας τῷ Ἰωσήφ (v. 18); πρὶν ἢ συνελθεῖν αὐτούς (v. 18); Ἰωσὴφ δὲ ὁ ἀνὴρ αὐτῆς (v. 19); ἐβουλήθη λάθρᾳ ἀπολῦσαι αὐτήν (v. 19); μὴ φοβηθῇς παραλαβεῖν Μαρίαν τὴν γυναῖκά σου (v. 20); παρέλαβεν τὴν γυναῖκα αὐτοῦ (v. 24); οὐκ ἐγίνωσκεν αὐτὴν (v. 25).

outcome from verse 16. According to verse 16, the outcome is that Jesus is the final heir, born from Mary whose husband is Joseph. So by verse 18 we already know that Mary and Joseph's marriage will work out somehow and that somehow Joseph will end up with Jesus as his heir despite not being produced, biologically, by Joseph himself.

What verse 16 did not tell us is *how* that outcome unfolded. The outcome in verse 16 requires an explanation because it is unexpected. Somehow Mary's husband is the man who is the legal father for a child that he did not produce in which two relational issues require an explanation, namely: (1) Joseph's relationship with Mary as husband; and (2) Joseph's relationship to Jesus as his assumed father. Verse 16 only presented the outcome without explaining the "how."

Therefore, verse 18 says "this is how it happened" (οὕτως ἦν). In other words, the final heir production (the Messiah being born into Joseph's lineage) happened in the following way. And so verse 18 begins to give the story. This is the missing story for which we already had been given the conclusion back in verse 16.

Note that verse 18 reintroduces the same two topical elements as verse 16, namely: the marriage relationship; and the paternal dilemma that Mary's child is not actually Joseph's offspring. When verse 20 mentions Joseph having resolved to do "these things" (ταῦτα) it is referring to the two things mentioned in the previous verse, namely: (1) not disclaiming Mary by publicly disclosing his nonpaternity; and (2) not claiming Mary as his wife.

Consequently, Matt 1:18a promises to tell the story of how these two issues were resolved, but we should not expect that verse 19 will suddenly conclude with the final outcome. The presented story cannot suddenly finish in the very next verse by having Joseph accept Mary as his wife and then name the born child. That would be to skip over, again, to the outcome without any "story" or without any explanation of how such an interesting outcome eventuated. What is required, in verses 19–24, is to explain how, even though it eventuated the way it did, we should actually expect either some kind of detour before arriving at that outcome or expect that the story will show other potential outcomes that almost eventuated.

So, by taking a cue from the story's preempted conclusion in verse 16 we can see that verse 18 sets us up for a story requiring an explanation for arriving at the eventual outcome (in other words the "how").

What this also means is that the story's newly expected outcome is the unexpected outcome given in verse 16 (and reiterated in verse 18). So Joseph is initially presented as resisting what has become the newly expected outcome and it is natural to expect Joseph, initially, to proceed to the older expected outcome, namely that he is unlikely to pose as the father for someone else's child. In other words, the astute audience is now expecting Joseph's initial plans to be at odds with the eventual outcome.

Unfortunately, if audience empathy with Joseph is not strong because the actual outcome is already known by readers and hearers, any plan Joseph begins to make that is not leading to it can seem "incorrect" to us. For this reason, those of us who skip the first seventeen verses and begin reading at verse 18 might potentially feel more empathy with Joseph than those of us who already know the outcome from verse 16 (at least until we see the overall pattern in the genealogy concerning the five fathers).

The story does indeed depict Joseph as doing something different from the story's own expected outcome but that does not mean that Joseph is resisting doing the right thing. I would now like to show how the text presents Joseph's intentions as essential to the story.

Unpacking Joseph's response (Matt 1:19)

We could pose the question this way: *How is it that Joseph can be presented as making a right decision both times even though his planned actions are opposite?* How is it that:

a. Joseph was right not to claim Mary and her child as his (vv. 18–19);

b. Joseph was right to claim Mary and the child as his (verses 24–25).

There is a text-based answer to unpack.

Greek-English Diglot (Matt 1:19)

Ἰωσὴφ δὲ ὁ ἀνὴρ αὐτῆς, δίκαιος ὢν καὶ μὴ θέλων αὐτὴν δειγματίσαι, ἐβουλήθη λάθρᾳ ἀπολῦσαι αὐτήν. SBLGNT	Joseph, her husband, being a righteous man and not willing to shame her, decided he would privately divorce her. (Matt 1:19)

Rather than simply saying, "Joseph decided he would divorce Mary," it includes several additional details that might seem unnecessary to mention. These details turn out to be extremely helpful for unpacking Joseph's plan.

Verse 19 begins by, again, identifying Joseph by name and then it unnecessarily adds the detail "her husband" (ὁ ἀνὴρ αὐτῆς) which we already know from verse 16 and from verse 18. Next it adds the detail "being righteous" (δίκαιος ὤν) then adds the intention "not to shame her" (μὴ θέλων αὐτὴν δειγματίσαι) then mentions a second intention "he decided" (ἐβουλήθη) and adds "quietly" (λάθρᾳ) to the plan "to divorce her" (ἀπολῦσαι αὐτήν). All of these additions are critical to unpacking the story.

Saying "her man" might initially seem to be a redundant detail. We already know that Joseph is the husband/man from verse 18 and also from verse 16. But it will gradually become clearer why it mentions that detail. For now, we can see that identifying Joseph as the man/husband puts the spotlight on Joseph as the one who is making a decision that will potentially affect the outcome of the story.

The added detail of Joseph "being righteous" is particularly informative since it functions as the only reason given for Joseph's plan (besides the additional clue when the angel mentions Joseph's fear). The description "being righteous" characterizes the kind of person Joseph is as the basis for Joseph's decision. Also it fits with the detail that Joseph decided to divorce Mary "quietly" which shows that it is not just about *what* he is planning to do but *how* he is going to do it. It concerns the ethical nature of his actions. The manner in which Joseph operates shows that he is sensitive to ethics as well as outcomes. The addition of "not wanting to shame her" displays Joseph's ethics of being discreet with what he knows could hurt Mary (namely that the child is not Joseph's child). Each added detail has the effect of slowing the story down to focus on Joseph's character.

It would be helpful to know exactly what it means in Matthew for Joseph to be introduced as being δίκαιος ("righteous") especially as this is the defining characteristic for understanding Joseph's intentions.

Though we could find various meanings in different contexts for the Greek word δίκαιος by seeing how different writers use the label (for example, Luke 1:6 gives us a definition of what it means for Elizabeth and Zechariah to be identified as "righteous") these other contexts may not fit perfectly with the context presented in Matthew 1. What we need is to look for another application within Matthew that seems most similar to Matthew 1.

There are general references in Matthew to "righteous ones" (for example, "sending rain on the righteous and the unrighteous," Matt 5:45; "the one who welcomes a righteous one in the name of a righteous one receives a righteous one's reward" Matt 10:41; and "many prophets and righteous ones longed to see what you see," Matt 13:17). But none of these are attached to a specific person, that is, a person who is a known character like Joseph in Matt 1:19.

There are only two other cases in Matthew where the term is applied to a named person: Jesus refers to Abel as δίκαιος (Matt 23:35); and Pilate's wife refers to Jesus as δίκαιος (Matt 27:19). Interestingly, in both of these cases it means "innocent."

In Matt 23:35, Jesus is quoted as referring to a known person, Abel (from Genesis 4) referring to "the blood of righteous Abel" (τοῦ αἵματος Ἄβελ τοῦ δικαίου) in which Abel is someone "innocent" who was murdered. In the Matthean context (Matt 23:29–31) it assumes that killing innocent people is something hypocritical since the perpetrators are, by definition, *not* innocent. Abel is the innocent victim identified as someone who was not guilty of the crime against him (death) since Abel did *not* provoke his brother and did not deserve death. Abel's brother is the hypocritical/guilty party.

Similarly, Pilate's wife tells Pilate not to prosecute "that righteous man [Jesus]" warning him, "Not [your business] for you and for that righteous man" (Μηδὲν σοὶ καὶ τῷ δικαίῳ ἐκείνῳ Matt 27:19). Here, Jesus is referred to as the innocent party who is not guilty of the charges (of threatening violence against the Temple). Pilate would be the guilty party if he participates in killing an innocent man.

The meaning "innocent" for δίκαιος (corresponding to the Hebrew צדיק) is not as unusual as we might suppose. There are two cases prior to Matthew in the scriptures where it means innocent/inculpable. In fact, these two prior occurrences are the only two cases in the scriptures where a named character is identified as "righteous" (Noah and Job).[3]

Noah is identified in Gen 7:1 as "righteous" (δίκαιος/צדיק) meaning Noah is "not guilty" of the kinds of activities of which his generation was guilty. Noah's generation is a corrupt generation but Noah is innocent of such crimes.

---

3. In Ezek 14:14, a third man comes close to being called a "righteous man" when suggesting that Daniel had "righteousness" ("Noah, Daniel and Job, through their righteousness").

Job, in the book of Job, suffers through difficult events and so his friends try to tell him that he must be guilty of doing something really bad to upset God. But no, despite what his friends assume, Job is innocent (Job 1:1).

What it means for a biblical character to be identified as δίκαιος/צדיק in these four cases is consistent. It characterizes a man by what he is not participating in or of what he is "not guilty." In both cases before Matthew 1 and in both cases later on in Matthew it identifies each man by what he is not inclined to do despite what it might look like according to the situation he ends up in. The basic meaning is "innocent" or "inculpable" with the implication of "atypical" since what the situation supposedly "looks like" (the man's context) does not help us predict the man's character because the usual assumptions do not apply.

It is not merely that Noah is not guilty of acting criminally once or twice. Noah had no *tendency* to do those things since he is *not that kind of man*. It identifies something about Noah's characteristic nature, in contrast to the characteristic nature of other men in his generation.

Likewise with Job, Job is presented as *not* being the kind of man that his friends assume he is. It means to say that Job was not inclined to do the sort of things that his friends assume that every man in Uz does.

Abel, likewise, is not culpable for his own death since he did not provoke his brother in any way. To assume Abel was responsible for the resulting sin would be to blame an innocent victim.

Similarly, Jesus is not a violent man threatening a violent uprising against the tyranny of Roman power despite what it might look like to the nervous authorities in Jerusalem. Jesus is not that kind of man.

In each case a character is identified as δίκαιος/צדיק in order to present a story about an *atypical* man. In each case, the man is not guilty of behaving the way people assume men generally behave within such a context. The men cannot, or should not, be determined by their situation or the how things ended for them. Assessing the man's character cannot simply be based on the usual assumptions. These four men are not representative of their respective contexts. Instead they function as exemplary figures by being "anti-examples" within each situation. Their stories are given in order to invite audiences into a greater "biblical" perspective. Noah, Job, Abel, and Jesus are not typical cases of typical men doing typical things in typical situations. Each atypical man's case functions as a way of judging what the typical men are doing by contrast. In Matt 27:19, Jesus is not the kind of person that those in power assume he is—he is *not* a violent man. That anyone would think he is reveals more about the kind of person who would make such an assumption. Prejudging such a man based on what a typical man must presumably be like is expressly being preempted by referring to him as δίκαιος.

So given all these cases, we might wonder how this helps with Matt 1:19. What is Joseph not guilty of doing? What is Joseph being falsely assumed to be like? How does the above definition apply in Joseph's case?

The long answer will become clearer throughout the book. The shorter answer can be seen in verse 19 in which Joseph is said to be avoiding the typical inclinations of other men. Immediately after being told he is δίκαιος, we find that Joseph would avoid what other men would not tend to avoid. Joseph would not be guilty of publicly disavowing or disclaiming Mary and would not be guilty of being married to Mary. Other men in Joseph's situation would not have been able to avoid one or the other. But in Joseph's case, the usual assumption of what other men would do does not apply.

The narrator might as well have said, "Do not assume, dear audience, that Joseph was inclined to do what you or other men would usually do in his situation. Joseph was not inclined to disclaim his paternity and disclaim Mary but nor was he inclined to claim Mary and to claim paternity for a child that was not his."

Another man in Joseph's situation, knowing he was not the father, may have been prone to say something about his lack of paternity and so inevitably end up disgracing Mary. Alternately, another man might easily feel entitled to Mary and her child even though whoever's child Mary is having has a greater claim. Joseph would do neither. It is an atypical response. Other men might have been jealous. Not only is Joseph not indiscreet he is also not jealous.

Joseph's plan will be difficult to do because it involves letting Mary go yet not telling anyone the reason why. Observing Joseph is to be reminded of what other men would not have avoided. According to the story, this double avoidance is δίκαιος, it is the least wrong (least culpable). He is an unexpected man with an unexpected plan (within a story vignette in which an audience expects the unexpected eventual outcome to be at odds with Joseph's initial plan).

It is the same principle at work whether Joseph considers Mary's pregnancy to be another man's child or to be God's own child. Whoever's child it is has a greater claim and should rightfully be known as the father. Joseph refuses to override that person's rightful claim to Mary and the child. For Joseph to claim Mary (and Mary's child) as his own would be a false claim. Joseph will not be culpable for doing such a thing.

We can now follow the situation as it unfolds. When the angel tells Joseph simply to go ahead ("Joseph, son of David, do not be afraid to take Mary your wife") the second part "your wife" (τὴν γυναῖκά σου) is somewhat redundant as there is a slight overlap between the two parts, namely between "do not be afraid to take Mary" and "[she is] your wife" since παραλαβεῖν Μαρίαν "to take Mary" can imply "take in marriage" ("take as wife").

The first part reflects awareness of Joseph's point of view. But the second part ("your wife") reflects a perspective that was not yet Joseph's perspective since Joseph does not consider Mary as *his* wife since Joseph has not yet "taken Mary" and she is already having someone else's child. By declaring that Mary *is* Joseph's wife the angel is formalizing the relationship (like a marriage celebrant would) and now Joseph need not "be afraid" (μὴ φοβηθῇς) to accept his own wife.

Interestingly, the Greek form of the word used for "take" is the same compound form used in Matthew 2 to tell Joseph to "take along" Mary and her child. Astute readers and hearers may already have noticed the compound form in Matthew 1. Is it being used differently in Matthew 1 ("take as your wife") from Matthew 2 ("take with you")? In the second case Joseph is being asked to take *along* his family *with* him). The same compound form is used for consistency to show a pattern in the kind of divine instruction as it will be repeated to Joseph in Matthew 2. But also, the idea of "taking that which is already yours" seems relevant to tell Joseph in Matthew 1. This compound form of "take" is what is usually used for receiving an inheritance or taking up a tradition or gathering up one's own possessions or relatives. As it appears in Matthew 1, the compound verb has a gentleness and naturalness about it—the mother of his heir can be *taken up/by/in/along/with* Joseph as a family member. Using the compound verb has the effect of softening an expression that might otherwise have sounded forceful or sexual, instead gently reminding us that Mary and Joseph belong together.

In fact, this is the fourth time that the story has stated that Mary and Joseph are (or should be) together. We were informed in verse 16 that Joseph was "the husband" and in verse 18 that Mary was his "betrothed wife." Again in verse 19 we were informed that Joseph was "the husband" and again in verse 20 from the angel that Mary is "Joseph's wife." The reiteration of togetherness is part of the persuasive technique at work encouraging us to notice the eventual tipping point when it begins to become a reality for Joseph rather than merely a statement of potentiality of what should happen. The angel's plan is about to be fulfilled. Then at the end of verse 24, we finally hear that "Joseph took along his wife!"

Perhaps the most striking feature of the divine instruction here is that the angel's plan appears to be consistent with what would soon be the public perception of Joseph's situation if he were *not* to influence the public opinion in anyway by *not* changing what it looks like. According to public perspective, Joseph and Mary will soon be considered husband and wife if Joseph does nothing differently and simply continues on with Mary. The angel is telling Joseph not to change this perception. In other words, Joseph is told to go along with the public perception in which Mary will be considered to be Joseph's wife. Not only is there no other husband competing for that role, her child is meant to be Joseph's heir making it the right thing to do in this case.

The angel is sanctioning the marital relationship (then sanctions the parental relationship in the following clauses). Ultimately, the angel is affirming what would naturally be, and what would become, the public perception. This is why we find the repeated affirmation of Joseph's and Mary's relationship (in verse 16 Joseph belongs to Mary; in verse 18 Mary belongs to Joseph; in verse 19 Joseph belongs to Mary; in verse 20 Mary belongs to Joseph; and in verse 24 Mary belongs with Joseph). So Mary and Joseph ultimately are meant to be together! That will be the accepted public opinion; that will become the story; and that is the outcome that the angel is sanctioning.

This can be verified by imagining what it would look like if it were completely opposite. We could imagine what the situation might be like if Joseph were planning to pursue the marriage after all and then the angel of the Lord intervened and said to Joseph, "Be afraid Joseph, be afraid for your life! You should not take Mary! She is not your wife!"

In fact, we do not even have to imagine what that opposite scenario would look like because we already have that exact scenario presented earlier in the scriptures. Back in the book of Genesis (Gen 20:3), God turns up in a dream to Abimelech and tells him to be afraid for his life because the woman he has taken is another man's wife. The story concerned Abraham and Sarah who had been telling everyone that they were only brother and sister. Consequently, King Abimelech took Sarah into his palace as a wife. Then God intervenes in a dream. Abimelech responds by declaring that he is "innocent" (δίκαιος/צדיק) since he had not begun a sexual relationship with Sarah and appealing to public opinion by saying that according to everyone, including Sarah herself, Sarah and Abraham were not husband and wife but brother and sister.

Abimelech's plea is unpersuasive to God. According to God's perspective in Genesis 20, God is saying that the public perception is wrong and cannot be relied upon for judging whether or not Abimelech really is considered "inculpable" (δίκαιος/צדיק).

Matt 1:20 depicts the opposite command given to Joseph as to that given to Abimelech in Gen 20:3. In Matthew 1, God instead interjects in order to *affirm* the public opinion. We find Joseph refusing to be culpable of taking Mary illegitimately then the divine perspective intervenes. Unlike Abimelech, Joseph is not relying on public opinion to determine his relationship status with Mary. Unlike Abimelech, Joseph is actually inculpable (δίκαιος/צדיק).

It is becoming clear what it was that Joseph was afraid of according to the story. Joseph was afraid of claiming Mary illegitimately even though it could look legitimate according to public opinion. Since Joseph was not depending on the public perception of Mary being his wife his "fear" is, appropriately, the fear of God/heaven. He *could* have claimed Mary as his wife (and claimed her child as his child) according to public opinion. But without divine permission it would not be right in the eyes of God. This is why divine permission is granted by the divine messenger who says, "Joseph, son of David, do not be afraid to take Mary your wife."

According to Matt 1:18–19, had Joseph simply taken Mary as his wife he would not have been atypical, he would have been a typical presumptuous man (without "fear of God"). In Gen 20, Abimelech learned that to fear/respect the public opinion was insufficient and was learning to fear/respect God's opinion (which Abraham thought was impossible; Gen 20:11). In Matthew 1, Joseph already fears God's opinion and he needs to be told that God is actually okay with the public opinion this time!

The role shaped for Joseph by the public is the role that God decides to affirm/sanction. In Genesis 20, the public perspective was offtrack so the divine perspective was needed. In Matthew 1, the public perspective, though inaccurate, was strangely enough on the right track. So the divine perspective was again needed yet for the opposite reason. Joseph was initially right *not to take Mary* for his wife (Matt 1:18–19) and then right *to take Mary* for his wife (Matt 1:24–25) once receiving divine permission.

In conclusion, Joseph's perspective is presented as differing from the audience's perspective as well as from the public perspective and then God's perspective intervenes to bring the various perspectives into alignment. We do not need to "undelete" an alleged missing/deleted scene in which Joseph confronts Mary asking about whose child it is. Joseph is presented as not presuming any rights to someone else's child (and to Mary). To import a scene where Joseph misjudges Mary or interrogates Mary is to miss the point of the story. The story does not present Joseph as taking that path or even needing to know such a thing. According to the story, what Joseph needed was not more human opinions about what seemed good for him to do in the eyes of other people, but rather he needed special guidance for a special case. The divine perspective reveals the future and permits Joseph to do what he would not otherwise have dared to have done.

In other words, the whole idea of Joseph incorrectly assuming something about Mary's behavior is a false start. Rather, the story is about Joseph not illegitimately presuming a role for himself out of jealous entitlement since Joseph is fearfully aware that the public perspective is deficient and is no grounds for claiming Mary and her child for himself. The text's audience discovers the real reason that Joseph "took" Mary and recognized the child as his own heir is not based on anything typical about the man Joseph and that it was God who sanctioned the public opinion on this occasion.

The story highlights Joseph's atypical response. The newly expected (previously unexpected) outcome that Jesus would or could be Joseph's heir (as known in verse 16 and verse 18 and eventuating in verse 25) does not occur without a detour with Joseph's character being naturally in tension with the story's seemingly illegitimate granting of paternity to Joseph, without which there would be no "how it happened" (v. 18a) or no "story conflict."

If the story of the divine intervention preventing Abimelech from taking Sarah as a wife is in the background, it becomes even more important to ask, "Why is Sarah not mentioned in the genealogy?" It seems that how Matthew 1 works overall still remains unclear. We still have a few more "what" questions to unpack in verses 18–25 before we can see how the story connects with the four previous references to mothers in Matthew 1.

6

What Kind of "Genesis" is it in Matt 1:18?

This chapter explores the concentric structure of verses 18–25 in order to understand the meaning of the first sentence ("The Jesus Messiah's progeneration was this way"). When the verse numbers are removed, the arrangement is easier to see. The center of the structure is, "This whole thing took place so as to fill up what was spoken by the Lord through the prophet." Either side of this is a pair of birth prophecies having four matching elements (notable pregnancy; birth of an heir; naming of heir; theological significance of name); either side of that is a pair of components with another four matching elements (angel; instruction; dream; decision); either side of that is a pair of components with matching elements (Joseph's potential and actual claiming of Mary); either side of that is a pair of components with matching elements (referencing Mary's status as mother and lack of sexual union); either side of that is the first and last sentences as matching components, revealing the kind of "progeneration" as a providentially-guided genesis achieved by human and divine cooperation. It turns out the heading to the unit is concise and informative.

IT WOULD BE HELPFUL to be able to unpack verse 18a, "The Jesus Messiah's genesis was thus" (Τοῦ δὲ Ἰησοῦ χριστοῦ ἡ γένεσις οὕτως ἦν). This heading appears as the first sentence in verse 18 introducing the remainder of the story unit (vv. 18b–25).

How is it an appropriate heading for a story about Joseph's dilemma and the revelation he receives? At first glance, this heading might not seem to be a very adequate description for the story unit. There are many things within the story that do not seem to be introduced by the heading. For example, the next few sentences outline Joseph's plan to divorce Mary as soon as he realizes she is pregnant with a child that is not his, which would, of course, jeopardize the child's Davidic inheritance. So Joseph is told to take Mary as his wife by an angel and given a prophecy telling him to call the child "Jesus" because "he is going to save his people from their sins."

If the story is about Jesus's messianic inheritance through Joseph and his divinely chosen name and mission, it might seem that the heading is not adequately descriptive for the story that it is supposed to be introducing, especially if we imagine that the heading is only referring to the "birth" of Jesus (as many English Bibles translate "genesis" here). But the birth itself is not detailed in the story (there is nothing about the day Jesus was born; no mention of when, where, or who was there). Consequently, most interpreters take the heading to be a vague reference to "circumstances of birth" (the circumstances surrounding or leading up to Jesus's birth). This might, at least, seem preferable to expecting a nativity scene in Matthew 1 that never eventuates (there is only a sort of "delayed" nativity scene in Matthew 2 set sometime afterward when Jesus is an infant under the age of two).

If we were hoping for a sentence that encapsulated everything that happens in verses 18–25 we would probably not choose this heading as it does not seem very descriptive. But why should it? Not all headings are particularly apt, clever, or interesting. Some headings are vague and nondescript.

However, it can be demonstrated from verses 18–25 that all the important aspects of the story unit are implied within the heading (the theme of inheriting Joseph; Jesus's divinely chosen name and mission; and Joseph's obedience to the divine agenda). This can be seen by making four observations: firstly, identifying what we expect the story will be about prior to verse 18; secondly, identifying the factors shaping the story; thirdly, identifying the single sentence that contains the coordinating factors of the story; and fourthly, identifying how the heading connects to that sentence.

The first thing to notice is that prior to verse 18 the previous two verses have encouraged us to expect that a particular kind of story will follow. Verse 17 comments on the structure of the Messiah's lineage highlighting how it was the right time for the Messiah to arrive, according to the structural "timing" of the genealogical groups of fourteen generations. In other words, it is not based on human timing but divine timing. So we might expect that what happens next is likewise going to outline something similar, namely divine timing or divine factors at work.

In verse 16, at the final "progeneration," Jesus was identified as the Messiah "born from Mary whose husband was Joseph." The piece that is conspicuously "missing" is the identification of *how the relationship worked out between Jesus and Joseph.* If Jesus is the final heir, the heir of Joseph, but Joseph is not the biological father of Jesus then what happened to make a parental connection of inheritance from Joseph to Jesus? A story awaits to be told of how Jesus became the heir, inheriting Joseph's lineage. Consequently, when we arrive at the heading in verse 18 it says, "The Jesus Messiah's progeneration happened like this," which means, "This is how Jesus was accepted into Joseph's Davidic lineage."

The second observation to make is to identify the contributing factors within the story itself. The influencing factors are: Joseph; Mary already being pregnant; the public opinion; the Holy Spirit; a prophecy from an angel of the Lord; and a scripture quotation. All of these factors are working together by the end of the story (both human and divine factors). The story outlines how these various factors converge bringing about the outcome by making Jesus the heir of Joseph son of David whose mission is to save his people from their sins.

The third observation is to identify a single sentence that contains this whole idea, namely the convergence of human and divine factors coming together to make Jesus the heir of Joseph tasked with this important mission. We might initially think that the prophecy given to Joseph is such a sentence ("the heir in her is from the Holy Spirit; she will give birth to a son; you will name him Jesus; for he will save his people from their sins") which is actually four sentences combined.

However, the short sentence at the end of the story unit contains the coordinating factors working together ("he called his name Jesus") since it was not Joseph's idea to "call his name Jesus" but it shows Joseph cooperating with the divine agenda in order to legitimate the father-son relationship. It simultaneously reflects the divine agenda at work while recalling the meaning of the name given to Joseph to give the child. In this one short sentence: Joseph is accepting Jesus as his son and thus into his Davidic lineage; it accords with a divine agenda; and the given name alludes to Jesus's life's mission of salvation as spoken in the prophecy.

The fourth thing to observe is how the final sentence might be connected with the first sentence, the heading. Is there any reason to see these two sentences as linked together or as referring to the same things? Yes. To see it means dividing up the story unit into separate components.

Unfortunately, the numbering of the verses we currently use prevents us from seeing the neat arrangement of sentences in Matt 1:18–25. When the verse numbers were added during the time of the early printing presses, the numbers were not made to correspond to separate sentences. For example, the verse currently numbered "18" contains two distinct sentences. It is difficult to identify all the carefully arranged sentences using our current verse numbers so these will need to be temporarily ignored in order to observe the structural arrangement.

The easiest way to spot the arrangement of sentences is to begin with the second of the two birth announcements ("Behold, the virgin will have a pregnant belly, and she will give birth to a son, and they will call his name Emmanuel, which means 'God is with us'"). These four sentences, or clauses, form a single component that parallels the birth announcement given to Joseph. The newer birth announcement given to Joseph is labeled "1" since it is mentioned first in the unit (Matt 1:20c–21).

Birth Announcement 1	Birth Announcement 2
For the heir in her is from the Holy Spirit	Behold, the virgin will have a pregnant belly
and she will give birth to a son	and she will give birth to a son
and you will call his name "Jesus"	and they will call his name "Emmanuel"
for he will save his people from their sins.	which means "God is with us."

Until the verse numbers are removed from view, it is easier to hear the parallels between the two annunciations than it is to see them. Having the same four-part structure, it is clear that both annunciations are intended to be matching components.

Between the two birth announcements there is a single sentence. This sentence is the center of the unit, around which every other component has a matching component on the opposite side. This symmetrical arrangement is known as "chiastic." The structure is also "concentric" since it contains a center component.

The birth announcement given to Joseph is the fifth component in from the heading (from the first sentence). The older birth announcement from Isaiah is the fifth component from the end (counting back from the final sentence of the unit).

Identifying the matching fourth components is now relatively easy. We might have considered separating the mention of the angelic messenger from the given message but the angelic command is apparently not considered to be separate according to the counterpart component where the same four elements are clearly together in a single sentence (re-solving to act; sleep; angel; and instruction). This means that all components consist of single sentences each except for the birth announcements which contain four short sentences each. Matching components are here labeled as "A" and "A'," "B" and "B'," and so on, with the center labeled "F." The concentric structure is:

A The progeneration of the Jesus Messiah was this way.

    B His mother Mary being betrothed to Joseph, before they came together, was already with a pregnant belly from the Holy Spirit.

        C Joseph, her husband, being righteous, and not wanting to shame her, decided he would quietly divorce her.

            D Having resolved to do these things, behold an angel of the Lord appeared to him in a dream saying, "Joseph son of David! Do not be afraid to take Mary, your wife."

                E "For the child is from the Holy Spirit, she will give birth to a son, you shall call his name Jesus, for he shall save his people from their sins."

                    F This whole thing occurred so as to be a fulfill-ment of that which was spoken by the Lord through the prophet:

                E' "Behold the virgin shall have a pregnant belly, she shall give birth to a son, they shall call his name Emmanuel—which, translated, is God-is-with-us."

            D' Joseph, rising from sleep, did as was commanded to him by the angel of the Lord.

        C' He took his wife.

    B' He was not knowing her up till the time she gave birth to a son.

A' He called his name Jesus.

Both "fourth components," (D being the fourth component from the beginning and D' the fourth from the end) contain the same four elements (angel of the Lord; instruction; resolution to put into action; and sleep/dream).

The next outer pair of components (C and C' being the third in and third from the end) identifies Joseph's relationship with the pregnant Mary (in C Joseph refuses to take Mary by not pursuing the relationship; in C', the counterpart sentence, Joseph does the opposite, namely he "takes" Mary).

The next outer pair of components, B and B' (the second in and second from the end) each contains a time-dependent clause concerning Mary and child, namely Mary's status as mother and having no marital relations with Joseph.

This leaves the first sentence and the final sentence as matching components, namely the consolidation of the father-son relationship by "adoption" not according to Joseph's own agenda but according to a divine agenda with the naming of Jesus identifying him in terms of his divinely given name (alluding to his messianic status as indicated in verse 21).

We can now unpack the first sentence ("The Jesus Messiah's progeneration was thus"). The "was thus" means "it happened this way," namely it refers to what eventuates. What eventuates is that Jesus, despite Joseph not being his biological father, becomes accepted as son of Joseph.

The "progeneration" or "genesis" here in Matt 1:18a is "of *the* Jesus Messiah." The definite article seems unnecessary when the name Jesus is combined with the title Messiah. Although some manuscripts omit the name Jesus and thus avoid the difficulty by simply saying "of the Messiah" (as in verse 17) the more difficult reading "of the Jesus Messiah" turns out to make good sense.

The first and final sentences within 18–25 highlight Jesus's acceptance by Joseph as Joseph's heir which simultaneously includes the divinely appointed name and mission. That is, it includes the messianic status bestowed on Jesus humanly (by Joseph) and divinely (by the angel of the Lord). This double legitimation, or dual causation, identifies the kind of progeneration previously introduced in verse 1. In other words, the meaning of the term γένεσις in verse 18a turns out to be not so different from its meaning in verse 1 in which it indicated heritage, distinct life (mission), and legacy.

Specifically, the unusual appearance of the definite article ("*the* Jesus Messiah's progeneration") would seem to be because it is referring back to the previous unit in verse 1 (βίβλος γενέσεως Ἰησοῦ χριστοῦ) and in verse 16 (ἐγεννήθη Ἰησοῦς ὁ λεγόμενος χριστός) in which the Messiah's own progeneration (γένεσις) was previously mentioned.[1] Verses 18–25 are about to explain how Jesus legally comes to be part of the previous lineage due to human as well as divine factors.

In other words, what is picked up from verse 1 and continued is the same topic—the topic of the "Jesus Messiah's progeneration" as the topic introduced in the first unit and explicated in the second unit. The topic includes the multiple aspects of "progeneration" identified in both units (messianic inheritance; title; name/mission; and legacy).

Determining Jesus's status as the chosen one is determined as a matter of divine providence clarified in the final sentence in which Jesus becomes heir to Joseph's lineage when Joseph gives Jesus the divinely determined name implying Jesus's mission of salvation. The process of divine legitimation involves Joseph's participation as part of a human-divine cooperation to make Jesus Joseph's heir.

In conclusion, the second unit of Matthew is comprised of careful internal interconnections. There is a clear link between the structure and meaning of verses 18–25. Its structure is what enables us to unpack its meaning. Without paying attention to the structure we would have struggled to discover the meaning of its heading.

The structural poetics of Matt 1:18–25 will be further explored in the following chapter, looking at the meaning of the middle of the unit, namely the middle sentence of the concentric structure (v. 22).

---

1. Comfort suggests it refers to "the birth of the Jesus just mentioned [in 1:16]." Comfort, *New Testament Text,* 4.

7

The Poetics of Fulfillment in Matt 1:22

Overview

This chapter examines the middle of the concentric structure in order to understand why verse 22 says, "All this has happened" seemingly before it has all happened. This refers to the previous component, namely the prophetic birth announcement, linking the two birth announcements together. When the two birth announcements are compared, we can observe how the newer one fills out the older one. There are various kinds of fulfillment/completion at work in the unit.

Greek-English Diglot (Matt 1:22)

τοῦτο δὲ ὅλον γέγονεν ἵνα πληρωθῇ τὸ ῥηθὲν ὑπὸ κυρίου διὰ τοῦ προφήτου λέγοντος	This whole thing occurred so that what was spoken by the Lord through the prophet would be filled up, namely . . .

FOR MANY OF US, verse 22 might seem out of place. It seems to be saying that everything has happened even before it has all happened. If Joseph has not yet named the child, Mary has not yet given birth, and Joseph is still asleep why does it say that it has already taken place? Consequently, many of us read it as if it means to say, "This *will* happen." This verse has confused commentators who might have preferred it to be placed at the conclusion of the story.

However, having now identified the structure of verses 18–25, we can see that it would not fit at the end of the unit. Since it is the middle component of the concentric structure and lacks a matching counterpart component, perhaps verse 22 is just a timeless remark floating outside the chronology of the unit?

Most commentators avoid the issue since it is presumably natural for the narrator to say something from a future perspective while looking back at the story being narrated. The whole thing did eventually happen so a narrator's perspective (as a future perspective) seems fair enough in verse 22 with a change of vantage points. If the previous sentences are narrated by presenting the perspective of the angel who is predicting what *will* happen and then the narrator's voice basically says "and (eventually) it did happen" then is this really a problem? It is only a problem for those who think it is the angel who continues to speak in verse 22. In that case, why the sudden shift from what *will* happen to what *has* happened, apparently before it has actually happened?

And what about the shift from plural to singular? The prophetic announcement given by the angel speaks of a plurality of things ("Mary will give birth to a son; you will call his name Jesus; he will save his people from their sins"). Then verse 22 speaks either of a single thing or an entirety of something, namely "this whole thing" (τοῦτο ὅλον). Several things are mentioned prior to verse 22 which together span different time frames (betrothal; pregnancy; intention to divorce) so we would not tend to think of all these things as a single thing (τοῦτο ὅλον). The following birth announcement that is "fulfilled" concerning the Emmanuel child likewise speaks of a plurality of things (pregnancy; birth; naming; legacy of Emmanuel) so why does verse 22 choose to speak simply of "this thing"? In other words, if these things have not yet happened, why does it present them as (a) having already happened and (b) as being one thing?

Four observations enable us to explain verse 22: (1) the observation that according to verse 22 something has already happened; (2) the observation that it is a singular thing; (3) the observation that it is an entire thing which contains parts within it; and (4) the observation of what previously, within the story, fits the above three observations.

It is easier to see what does not fit the criteria, namely what is in the second sentence which tells of Mary and Joseph's relationship and Mary's pregnancy. Both the marital status and pregnancy are presented as being incomplete. "Before they came together" presents an incomplete marriage. Likewise Mary's pregnancy presents Mary as an expecting mother so the pregnancy has yet to come to completion. Neither of these things fit the first criterion. Similarly, in the third sentence Joseph is presented as making a plan which is incomplete because it has not yet been enacted.

The answer begins to appear in the fourth sentence, which speaks of something that has happened, namely an angel appeared to Joseph and has given him a message ("behold an angel of the Lord appeared to him a dream saying, 'Joseph son of David do not be afraid to take Mary your wife'"). Joseph has now been given an instruction about being married to Mary. Then, in the next sentence, the angel gives Joseph a four-part prophecy about the child.

Notice that the message given to Joseph is a thing, having parts within it, yet being a singular thing as something that has just happened. Why have we not previously noticed that the divine speech is "this whole thing" that "has taken place"?

We probably have not noticed this because of our tendency not to think of speech as something active that "happens" or "takes place." Yet speeches are things that do happen; a speech is an act, especially divine speech according to biblical texts. So "this whole thing" (τοῦτο δὲ ὅλον) refers to "this whole speech" (or "this whole prophecy") which γέγονεν "happened" or "took place" (we would probably say "was given" in English).

As the middle sentence of the concentric structure, verse 22 is itself concentrically structured:

> This whole (thing) occurred
>> so as to fulfill
> what was spoken by the Lord through the prophet

> τοῦτο δὲ ὅλον γέγονεν
>> ἵνα πληρωθῇ
> τὸ ῥηθὲν ὑπὸ κυρίου διὰ τοῦ προφήτου λέγοντος·

The first and third elements are balanced counterparts such that the thing spoken to Joseph corresponds to the thing spoken by the Lord through the prophet (the prophet Isaiah being quoted in verse 23). The two prophetic speeches are linked together such that the more recently occurring one (given through an angel) is like a new version of the older one (given through Isaiah). In the middle of verse 22 is an expression of "fulfillment" (to be filled up; filled out; completed). Verse 22 is explaining why Joseph received such a prophecy by linking it with the older prophetic speech. So "this whole thing" refers to what was spoken to Joseph (by the Lord's angel) as filling out what was previously spoken by the Lord through the prophet

(Isaiah). Readers and hearers are invited to compare the two prophecies. The announcement previously given in Isaiah is filled out by the announcement more recently given to Joseph.

On the one hand, this solution seems pretty obvious since we already knew that the invitation was to compare the two birth announcements. However, one issue that is not fully resolved is whether we should include the first part of the angel's speech instructing Joseph to be married to Mary within "this whole thing." Does "this whole thing" include the marital instruction or does it refer only to the four-part birth announcement?

This question resolves itself when we follow the invitation to compare the two birth announcements. The birth announcement that is narrated first is the one more recently given to Joseph (Matt 1:21) and the birth announcement mentioned second is the one previously given back in Isaiah to King Ahaz (Isa 7:14). King Ahaz is one of the ancestors of Joseph mentioned in verse 9 so both birth announcements are given to descendants within the same lineage.

The older birth announcement given to Ahaz is notably ambiguous. It is a strange birth announcement since there is no identification of who the child's parents are and consequently who exactly the child is. By contrast, it is much clearer who the child's mother is (and who will be considered the child's father) in the case of the more recent birth announcement given to Joseph. Thus one aspect that is being "filled up" (or "filled out") in the more recent birth announcement is that the identification of parentage is more fully defined. Interestingly, neither recipient was expecting a birth announcement.

The older birth announcement is being interpreted for the audience in light of the newer one. It is not that we are encouraged to collapse the two together, as if there is only one birth announcement to consider. Rather, readers and hearers are offered a way to compare the two by reading the newly given annunciation as an extrapolation of the older annunciation in Isa 7:14, the new as an elaboration of, or fuller expression of, the old.

Note that the more recent birth announcement is given to Joseph as the reason for the marriage instruction (γὰρ). Joseph is not simply instructed to be married to Mary; he is given an instruction along with a prophetic birth announcement as the reason to follow the instruction.

The same pattern can be observed in the older birth announcement. In the case of the older annunciation in its context in the book of Isaiah, King Ahaz was given a birth announcement as the supporting reason to follow an instruction. This helps to answer the question about whether to include the previous instruction as part of the "whole thing" that has taken place. Even though the thing being compared and filled out is the prophetic birth announcement and not the instruction, the announcement to Joseph is presented as the reason to follow the previous instruction. Coincidentally, this was also the way the older birth announcement worked in Isaiah.

Thus both annunciations were given to encourage the recipient to follow an instruction and both instructions were intended to change the recipient's plan. In the case of King Ahaz he was about to make an alliance with Assyria and the given instruction from the Lord is for him to stop (and not to do his own plan). The annunciation to Ahaz is then given as an encouragement to follow the divine instruction. Similarly, the instruction given to Joseph is to prevent his own plan and replace it with a divine plan.

Note that what is also being filled up or filled out is that there is an improved efficiency with which the instruction is received. As a recipient, Joseph is much more receptive than was Ahaz who was not interested in following his instruction. Ahaz did not want any encouragement to follow the instruction and so was not encouraged by the birth announcement. In the case of Joseph, there is no detectable resistance to the instruction. Instead, the newer annunciation functions in a new and improved way, presenting Joseph as receptively obedient to the instruction and receptively encouraged by the birth announcement.

As seen in the previous chapter, when we compare the two birth announcements we find that each annunciation has the same four elements, occurring in the same order.

Birth Announcement to Joseph	Birth Announcement from Isaiah
For the heir in her is from the Holy Spirit	Behold, the virgin will have a pregnant belly
and she will give birth to a son	and she will give birth to a son
and you will call his name "Jesus"	and they will call his name "Emmanuel"
for he will save his people from their sins.	which means "God is with us."

The matching components enable a comparison to be made between each one of the corresponding four parts. The first part in each identifies that a significant birth will soon take place. The second part identifies a son born. The third identifies the name given. The fourth identifies the significance of that name for the people.

Interestingly, in the first part of the more recent annunciation given to Joseph, the subject is not the mother but the heir whom the mother is carrying. It seems Mary does not need to be identified to Joseph so it is identifying the child as Joseph's heir rather than identifying the mother. In the older annunciation, the mother is only vaguely identified by a descriptor (the virgin/the bride) as though the more important point was to get to the name of the child rather than to clarify the mother's identity. We can infer that the two identities of the two heirs are noteworthy and somehow comparable. Thus the child Mary is having is like the child the virgin is having.

In the third parts of the two annunciations, the given birth names differ. In the case of the older annunciation given to Ahaz the name given is Emmanuel whereas, in the more recently given annunciation to Joseph, the name is Jesus. The way the naming of Emmanuel is presented in Matthew diverges from the usual Greek and Hebrew use of pronouns (in Isa 7:14) by instead saying "*they* will call him" which, in Matthew, now emphasizes the communal nature of the name. This divergence enables an audience to think of Emmanuel as a name given by the people thereby allowing it to be applicable also to Jesus.

In the two fourth parts we are presented with the meanings of the respective names. "God is with us" is applicable to Ahaz's time (for the near future events about to happen) and it is also, apparently, applicable to Jesus since it alludes to a later generation of readers and hearers who believe that Jesus being with them means also that God is with them (see Matt 28:20). The corresponding identification between the presence of Jesus and the presence of God increasingly becomes more theologically significant in later generations.

The name Jesus (Ἰησοῦς) is not a Greek name but a Hebrew name. Ancient readers and hearers would presumably know that Jesus's name does not have a meaning in Greek (similarly, all the names cited in verses 2–16 are Hebrew names not Greek names). It refers to the Hebrew meaning of Jesus's name according to the Hebrew name "Yehoshua" ("YHWH saves") when it draws out the significance of his name.

Like several other Hebrew names, Yehoshua (יְהוֹשׁוּעַ) is "theophoric," that is, it includes within it an element of God's Hebrew name meaning that some readers and hearers who do not know any Hebrew would miss the ambiguity of the pronoun "he" in the explanation of the name in verse 21. The pronoun in "he will save" could be referring either to Jesus *or* to God who will save. The ambiguity is lost on audience members unfamiliar with Hebrew names and who can only guess that the Hebrew name probably relates somehow to "salvation."

The same kind of ambiguity continues with the pronoun "his" in "his people." Will it be Jesus's people being saved or will it be God's people? The ambiguity creates an overlapping reference where it is possible to read it one way or the other or both ways for those who know that some Hebrew names, like Yehoshua, refer to God's divine name.

This means that in both annunciations, both names (Emmanuel and Jesus) imply an overlap of human and divine activities. Just as the people would recognize God's presence and activity working among them in the life of Emmanuel, the same can be said concerning the life of Jesus. If the audience missed the human-divine overlap in the explanation of Jesus's name they could still perceive it when comparing the matching birth announcements.

Even though the middle component does not have a matching component, it is tied to the preceding and following components (namely the fifth component in and the fifth component from the end) so that unpacking the two fifth components simultaneously unpacks the middle component. It is almost impossible to examine the middle component (Matt 1:22) by itself because "this whole thing" refers to the preceding birth announcement and "the given oracle from the Lord" refers to the following mention of the older birth announcement from Isa 7:14 (Matt 1:23). What "has happened" is that the older annunciation has now been "filled out" by the newer. What fills out the older birth prophecy is another birth prophecy.

Finally, note the many kinds of completion at work. The divine speech completes a divine instruction. The prophecy of the heir's destiny is presented as the reason for the instruction to be married to Mary. The identification of the child to be born is much clearer in the newly given divine speech, presenting a more complete portrait or a fuller picture of who is the mother as well as who is the child about to be born. Joseph is a much more receptive kind of recipient compared to the first time around where the recipient, Ahaz, was not very receptive so Joseph's fuller receptivity makes the divine speech more complete. The most prominent kind of completeness is that the divine speech is expressly labeled as completed, not only using the vocabulary of "fulfillment" (ἵνα πληρωθῇ) but also the language of "happened" (γέγονεν).

If we were to skip from the first three components to the final three components (skipping over the middle five components) what remains is a contrast between potentialities and eventualities. The first three components present potentialities while the final three components present the corresponding eventualities. That is, the first three components outline several unfulfilled realities of which the final three components present as enacted. Interestingly, the expression "be fulfilled" (ἵνα πληρωθῇ) is reserved for the middle component, specifically the middle of the middle component.

The middle five components present a process of transition of completeness that begins immediately after Joseph has "resolved to do these things." Understandably, the story unit does not jump straight from unfulfilled potentiality to materialized reality. The process of actualization begins in the fourth component. The final three components present the materialized outcome of the previously incomplete marriage between Mary and Joseph; of Mary's expected pregnancy; and of Joseph's planned action. However, when these are resolved in the final three components they are depicted as completed without the specific language of completion used (it is reserved for the divine speech). It is the transitional component which is designated as that which completes or fulfills.

The middle consists of the five middle components (D, E, F, E′ D′) where the transformation is depicted as taking place:

A The progeneration of the Jesus Messiah was this way.

   B His mother Mary being betrothed to Joseph, before they came together, was already with a pregnant belly from the Holy Spirit.

      C Joseph, her husband, being righteous, and not wanting to shame her, decided he would quietly divorce her.

         D *Having resolved to do these things, behold an angel of the Lord appeared to him in a dream saying, "Joseph Son of David! Do not be afraid to take Mary, your wife."*

            E *"For the child is from the Holy Spirit, she will give birth to a son, you shall call his name Jesus, for he shall save his people from their sins."*

               F *This whole thing occurred so as to be a fulfillment of that which was spoken by the Lord through the prophet:*

> E' *"Behold the virgin shall have a pregnant belly, she shall give birth to a son, they shall call his name Emmanuel—which, translated, is God-is-with-us."*
>
> D' *Joseph, rising from sleep, did as was commanded to him by the angel of the Lord.*
>
> C' He took his wife.
>
> B' He was not knowing her up till the time she gave birth to a son.
>
> A' He called his name Jesus.

The five middle components present the intermediate section as an intermediate state of "becoming," namely a liminal state transitioning between two states, before and after the divine speech. Sleep is appropriate here as an intermediate state potentially more receptive to divine interaction.

Also fitting is that the intermediate section is transformed by a divine intermediary. The divine intermediary reveals a future state thereby bringing the future into the present, conjoining the two.

Here the very factors which seemed to be in tension with one another merge into a cooperative union. The differing perspectives between Joseph and the public coalesce with the divine perspective when the divine speech brings everything together.

Joseph is instructed by the angel to be married to Mary because (γὰρ) the child Mary is carrying is Joseph's future heir (τὸ ἐν αὐτῇ γεννηθὲν) and Joseph needs to know the appropriate name to give the child. To Joseph is revealed the child's name and the child's future but why is the revelation presented as a four-part birth announcement formula? The angel could have simply told Joseph what to do. Instead, Joseph is emboldened with not only an instruction but a birth announcement formula. The reason for this (τοῦτο δὲ ὅλον γέγονεν ἵνα) is to match his own situation in which he too has just noticed (Ἰδοὺ) that his betrothed woman (ἡ παρθένος) is evidently pregnant (ἐν γαστρὶ ἕξει) by giving him a revelation in biblical style because it not only helps Joseph to know what happens next (and whether he has any role in it) it tells the audience what happens next according to what already had been told to Ahaz about what happens next. The revelation to Joseph is, appropriately, presented as a biblical revelation in sync with an older revelation.

It is the divine speech which expresses both a potential reality and brings into fulfillment the materialization of a potential reality. The divine speech is what brings about the shift in order to bring things together by integrating Joseph's potentiality with Joseph's reality. The pivot of the story is this shift into completion. Hence, the story hinges on the double annunciation with the concept of completion holding center place.

In conclusion, structurally, verse 22 completes the story unit by identifying how things transition from being expressly unresolved into expressly resolved. So the newer birth announcement is not unprecedented but displays a consistency of the sort of thing that God has said in the past. The continuity between the two birth announcements is a kind of completeness, by showing a consistency in the continuation of an old idea being "filled out" and "filled up." According to the story unit, what fills out prophetic speech here is more prophetic speech, with the revelation to Joseph building on the revelation given to his ancestor Ahaz, heir of David.

Whilst the structure is beautifully symmetrical and the content is inextricably tied to that structure, we still have not unpacked how the second unit completes the first unit. What is being completed in verses 18–25 is ultimately what began in the first unit. It must still be explained how the story of Jesus being accepted by Joseph relates to the previous account of his ancestral lineage, particularly as it relates to the first four highlighted paternities. How is the story of Jesus becoming Joseph's son meant to complete the previous account of messianic ancestry?

8

How Matt 1:18–25 Completes Matt 1:1–17

Overview

This chapter reiterates the critical connections between the second unit (vv. 18–25) and the first unit (vv. 1–17) in order to clarify how the two units are meant to function interdependently as a whole. This is necessary to make clear so as to leave little room to doubt that the fifth highlighted case is meant to be connected with the previous four highlighted cases. Several points previously mentioned are here brought together. Both units purposefully share almost identical headings. The second heading is not the first time that the topic of "how" has been raised in Matthew 1. Verse 17 had addressed the topic of "how" by showing how the timing of the Messiah's arrival was providential. Verse 16 highlighted the absence of "how" Joseph's heir could be Jesus, which verse 18 then asserts to explain. The twin headings (v. 1 and v. 18a) are meant to identify the same topic of how the Messiah's progeneration came about. Verse 16 looks forward to the explanation and back to the previous four highlighted stories where the topic of "how" particular heirs were produced was highlighted. Each reference is a reference to an identifiable story in which the audience could be expected to say, "Yes we know that particular story!" leading the audience to see how the heirs were procured by the respective patriarchs.

OBSERVING THE STRUCTURAL SYMMETRY at work in the second unit (vv. 18–25) might tempt us to consider these verses only in isolation from the preceding unit (vv. 1–17). Some commentators might even doubt that the two units are meant to work together as a single "chapter" of Matthew.

To modern audiences, both units together obviously make what we call the first chapter of Matthew. But since it was not until the thirteenth century that Stephen Langton added the modern/standard chapter divisions it pays to examine the internal support for supposing that Matt 1:1–25 reflects a whole "chapter."

As it turns out, both units are apparently working towards a single common goal by means of a series of shared features. Note the following commonalities.

Both units present Jesus as the final heir to a royal lineage by identifying him as Messiah (χριστός), a term that is not often used in Matthew but is the central proclamation in both units of Matthew 1, namely Jesus arrives at the end of a royal lineage from David and from Abraham. The birth prophecy that Joseph receives continues an earlier birth prophecy given to Joseph's ancestor, King Ahaz, mentioned in the first unit (v. 9). Just as Ahaz was addressed as "House of David" (Isa 7:13) Joseph is addressed as "Joseph son of David." Both recipients answer to the name David as heirs to the same royal lineage and both are recipients of a royal birth announcement. As the final heir, Jesus's mission will not be the usual one of begetting biological offspring to produce more heirs; he arrives at the end of the line with a unique purpose.

Both units, conspicuously, share an almost identical heading.

> First heading (v. 1):
>
> Βίβλος γενέσεως Ἰησοῦ χριστοῦ υἱοῦ Δαυὶδ υἱοῦ Ἀβραάμ
>
> Book of the progeneration of Jesus Messiah, son of David, son of Abraham

> Second Heading (v. 18a):
>
> Τοῦ δὲ Ἰησοῦ χριστοῦ ἡ γένεσις οὕτως ἦν
>
> Of the Jesus Messiah's progeneration it was thus

The audience is notified that what is being narrated in the second part of Matthew 1 concerns the same providential "progeneration" of the final heir introduced in verse 1 (βίβλος γενέσεως) and the second heading then offers to explain "how it was" (οὕτως ἦν), namely the "progeneration." That is, how Jesus can be legitimately identified as the final heir in this messianic lineage is being specified.

The similarity of the two headings tends to go unnoticed in English Bibles where they are often translated very differently as if the first heading were merely genealogical (translating genesis as "genealogy") and as if the second heading were referring to Jesus's birth (translating genesis as "birth"). While it is accurate to say that Jesus is born in the second unit it is also accurate to say that Jesus is born in the first unit ("from Mary Jesus was born," v. 16). In fact, both units present, very briefly, the birth of Jesus near the end of the unit but not as the final component. In both units Jesus is born and then named ("the one called Messiah," v. 16; "he called his name Jesus," v. 25). The naming in the first unit signals the culmination of a lineage and distinguishes the kind of person arriving to perform a distinct role. Similarly, in the second unit the naming evokes the significance of a distinct messianic mission.

Both units of Matthew 1 emphasize that the final heir to the royal lineage arrived as a progression of a providentially-guided process. The process of progressing to, and arriving at, the final heir is no mere human accomplishment. The second unit presents this providential process by identifying the Holy Spirit and an angel of the Lord who gives a divine instruction and birth prophecy connected to an older prophecy from Scripture. In the first unit, providential guidance is highlighted in verse 17 with the timing of the Messiah's arrival reflecting supernatural guidance as well as being identified in verse 1 in which the process is identified as βίβλος (a sacred story; a providentially guided account). Arriving at the final heir is more than an ordinary process according to both units.

Mary, the mother of the Messiah, is mentioned in both units. It is not that Mary is mentioned merely because Joseph's active role as producer was omitted, as if the writer had no choice but to mention Mary. The writer could have ended the lineage by saying, "Jacob produced Joseph to whom was born Jesus."

The presence of Mary and the earlier mention of mothers in the first unit all belong to the same kind of connection as the other shared features between the two units. The mention of mothers is related to the way that the lineage progresses in order to arrive at the final heir by highlighting five cases in an overall extraordinary process.

All these shared features are there to help articulate a common goal, that is, the process of getting to the final heir. In other words, every one of these common features is concerned with the topic of how Jesus came to be the final heir.

In order to identify why mothers are mentioned in the way they are, it is important to begin with a question that is a lower level question than a "why" question. A "how" question is an intermediate level question between the higher "why" question and the lower level "who," "what," "when," and "where" questions. The "how" includes elements of "who," "what," "when," and/or "where." It is necessary to pay attention to the intermediate "how" question because, in Matthew 1, the topic of "how" is highlighted seven times prior to the second unit.

The second unit expressly refers to how the messianic progeneration happened, saying, "how it happened" (οὕτως ἦν) at the beginning of verse 18. It should also be noted that the same topic already appeared in the very first verse concerning the final heir arriving, that is, his "progeneration" as well as in verse 17 (how the timing of arrival was timed providentially). In fact, the topic of how also appeared five more times when particular mothers were referenced. Each reference to a mother modified the linear heir production by specifying *how* the heir was produced (*from a mother* in five cases).

When in verse 18 it says that this is *how* the final heir progeneration happened, it continues the topic of "how" from verse 16 (Joseph's heir produced from Mary *but somehow not by Joseph*) thereby continuing the topic from the previous mention of how heirs were progenerated by Judah from Tamar (v. 3), by Salmon from Rahab (v. 5), by Boaz from Ruth (v. 5) and by David from her of Uriah (Bathsheba, v. 6). In other words, the prepositional phrase "from a mother" is an adjunct that modifies the verb so as to identify the circumstances in which the progenitor "produced."[1]

In this way, the unanswered question of "how" opened up at verse 16 is answered in verses 18–25 but it is also linked back to the preceding mentions of how heirs were produced (from the three named mothers, Tamar, Rahab, and Ruth and from "her of Uriah," Bathsheba). When Mary is mentioned at the end of the genealogy, it is the fifth reference to a mother of an heir. Mary's presence in the first unit is a two-way connection (looking forward and looking back). It is in verse 16 that we find the most overlap between the two units.

Audiences are not encouraged to consider exactly how every heir in the lineage was produced prior to verse 18 since it is difficult to perceive many individual narrative events due to the rapid pace of the process of begetting heirs. The exceptions are the five cases where the narration slows down just enough to consider how particular heirs were produced.

---

1. Adjuncts provide "answers to questions of the type 'where?', 'when?', 'why?' and 'how?' [highlighting] the circumstances associated with the process." O'Donnell et al., "Clause Level Annotation Specification."

The second unit begins by reintroducing Jesus, Mary, and Joseph whereas the first unit had already introduced Joseph, Mary, and Jesus, that is, the order in which they appear is reversed. In the first unit, Jesus was identified in terms of his status as the final heir in verse 16 (χριστός), Mary was identified as Jesus's mother (Μαρίας, ἐξ ἧς ἐγεννήθη), and Joseph was identified in terms of his relationship to Mary (τὸν Ἰωσὴφ τὸν ἄνδρα Μαρίας). These same three identifications appear at the beginning of the second unit, identifying Jesus as the final heir (χριστός), Mary as his mother (τῆς μητρὸς αὐτοῦ Μαρίας), and Joseph as the one to whom Mary is betrothed in marriage (μνηστευθείσης τῷ Ἰωσήφ). The reappearance and reversal of the three names, along with the same relational identifications indicate an interlinking of both units.

Every time that a mother is referenced it effectively introduces two new relationships to consider. Along with the father-son relationship it introduces a mother-son relationship as well as a marital/conjugal relationship. Thus rather than simply the father-son (progenitor-heir) relationship there are three relationships implied (actually more than three in the case of Bathsheba who is also identified as "Uriah's").

Conversely, in the basic formula where mothers are not mentioned there is only a single father-son relationship as the linear progression from ancestor to heir, without any reference to "how" an heir was produced.

The five highlighted cases of how particular heirs came about are not all presented in an identical way in Matthew 1. In the final case, the heir is mentioned after the mother is mentioned. In the fourth case, the mother is unnamed and the name of her husband is mentioned. By comparison, the third case looks more straightforward. The second case also appears to be a straightforward reference to a story yet there is no such story mentioning Salmon in the scriptures, only a story about Rahab. In the first case, two sons are named.

We might be disappointed with these differences in referencing and take it as a sign that the five stories are not all meant to be connected as a group. However, rather than see these variations as detracting from the whole, we might see them as adding supplementary aspects for the kind of observations to consider when thinking of all five stories. In other words, the variations can clue us in to various angles to consider about these stories. We might notice, for example, that mentioning the twin sons born to Tamar reflects that the story ended well as a good result from a complex and less than ideal situation. Despite initial difficulties for both Judah and Tamar, the story ended well, with *two* sons born. The same kind of observation might help us with all five stories and is perhaps most obvious in the fifth case in which the produced heir is the one called Messiah, indicating a very good outcome.

Likewise, the inclusion of Bathsheba's husband introduces another kind of triangulation in the relationships concerning how the heir was produced, namely Bathsheba's child could potentially have been Uriah's child. The idea of ambivalent paternity might also be a relevant angle to consider in the other four cases.

This means that the five highlighted cases are not only presenting simple "triangles of relationships" when introducing relationships of mother-son and parent-parent relationships. More complex "triangles" are included, leading to more complex angles to consider.

Verse 16 not only implies that there is an unknown/untold story to follow ("how it happened" in verse 18), it also implies that the previous references to mothers are the *known* stories with which to compare the final heir production.

But what about the mothers, like Sarah and Rebecca, who are not referenced? Apparently, those stories are omitted because they do not accord with the kind of pattern being highlighted in the five cases. Also, they are not easy to summarize in terms of *how*. Consider what the effect would have been had Sarah been included as if it had said, "Abraham produced Isaac *from Sarah*." In this case, it would have had the effect of intending to highlight how it was that Abraham procured Isaac as his heir as a result of a long series of story vignettes, taking place over the course of many chapters in the book of Genesis (chapters 11–22) including a rival heir (Ishmael) who Abraham produced from Hagar (a story in which Sarah plays a critical role in desperately trying to obtain an heir for Abraham). It is not that the series of stories of procuring Isaac as an heir from Sarah are less well known or less unusual or less extraordinary but there are just too many story vignettes to consider for identifying a simple process of how Abraham procured Isaac as his heir. Mentioning Sarah would not have clearly specified any one story in particular. Readers and hearers are not being expected to think of all the various stories about Sarah and/or attempt to merge the stories into a single story.

Likewise, there are several stories concerning the production of Isaac's heir in which Rebecca plays a significant role in determining how Jacob becomes the chosen heir of Isaac. Had Rebecca been mentioned it could potentially bring different stories to mind for different readers and hearers. And which particular story was supposed to come to mind if all the mothers were mentioned from whom Jacob produced Judah and his brothers? The available options would have presented too much variety and complexity to make the point clear and easily connectable to other stories.

By contrast, the stories of the mothers referenced in the genealogy are more easily identifiable because they are each presented as being single stories, making it easy for readers and hearers to identify each story of heir production from the references to those mothers in the scriptures so as to identify what is being highlighted when Tamar, Rahab, Ruth, and Uriah's wife (Bathsheba) are referenced. Readers and hearers can be expected to say, "Oh we know that story!" and therefore to be able to notice the overall pattern of how these heirs were produced.

Another way of saying all this is to say that the two biggest literary questions in Matthew 1 both have the same answer. That is, the question of how the first unit can be called Jesus's progeneration (γένεσις) and the question of why there are five references to mothers in the ancestry both have the same answer. *How* Jesus arrives as the product of this ancestral lineage simultaneously answers both questions.

The following chapter examines what is so relevant to notice about the first highlighted heir production, namely how Judah produced Perez and Zerah from Tamar. It will then become apparent why Matt 1:18–25 does not focus on the mother-son relationship even though, potentially, it could have been a story about Mary and Jesus. Instead, verses 18–25 focus on how the father-son relationship worked out as it did. Note that this is the same focus presented in the first unit whenever mothers are referenced.

Having already studied the fifth case (in chapters 5, 6, and 7) and having noticed that Joseph's intentions toward Mary were critical to the story, it will now be easier to look out for a similar part in the first highlighted story by observing Judah's intentions toward Tamar.

9

The Parallel Scene to Matt 1:18–25
in Gen 38:24–26

Overview

This chapter looks at how the first and fifth highlighted stories of heir productions are meant to correspond, looking at the moment in the story of Judah and Tamar when Judah finds out that Tamar is pregnant. The story parallels the story of Joseph finding out that Mary is pregnant in which a betrothed woman is waiting for the man to accept her into his household; the man discovers the woman is already pregnant; the man does not know who is the father of the woman's child (he presumes a lack of his own paternity); the man makes a decision about what to do; that decision is then overridden by a revelation of new information; and the outcome is that the man is surprisingly conferred with the status of paternity. Furthermore, just prior to the narration of the birth of offspring the same expression is used in both stories ("he did not know her"). The point of the similarities is to compare each man's initial response within the same kind of story vignette. In both cases, the story functions as a type of "recognition scene" of surprise paternity.

Greek-English Diglot (Matt 1:3)

Ἰούδας δὲ ἐγέννησεν τὸν Φαρὲς καὶ τὸν Ζάρα ἐκ τῆς Θαμάρ	Judah progenerated Perez and Zerah from Tamar

WE DO NOT NEED to look very far for a story parallel to Matt 1:18–25. Theoretically, we could explore "parallel" stories not mentioned in Matthew 1 from other Second Temple literature in which paternity for a child in an important lineage was the topic. In the first century, there were stories circulating

103

about Moses's father almost divorcing Moses's mother (Jochebed) just before Moses was conceived, thereby jeopardizing Moses ever being born. Likewise, there were stories about Noah's father Lamech not wanting to claim Noah as his son, thinking that Noah's mother (Bathenosh) had been unfaithful to him with one of the rogue angelic beings (according to a popular interpretation of Gen 6:1–5 as presented in 1 Enoch).

However, these are not the parallels expected to come to mind for the earliest audience of Matthew 1 because the first unit of Matthew has already referenced four parallel stories with which to compare the story of how Joseph surprisingly gained his status of paternity. The first parallel story is found in the first mentioned heir production to include a mother in verse 3, that is, "Judah produced Perez and Zerah from Tamar." This is the parallel story that readers and hearers would first be expected to notice. The parallels are so striking that it is astonishing that commentators have not previously studied them. One intriguing element is the linguistic parallel that appears just prior to the respective mothers giving birth ("he did not know her") in each case. If the other connections have not been studied, this linguistic parallel might seem like a curious coincidence.

The reference to Tamar is found in Matt 1:3 after the first three heir productions have only mentioned that the father produced a son. The pace of the progression from Abraham to Isaac to Jacob moves swiftly then slows down at Judah. In reading aloud the third heir production (Jacob produced Judah *and his brothers*) the progression first slows down with Judah by the addition of "and his brothers." It then slows down again with the mention of a second named son (Judah produced Perez *and Zerah*). Then, for a third time, slows down with the mention of how it was that this came about (*from Tamar*). Whereas Isaac's other son (Jacob's twin brother Esau) had remained unmentioned, Perez's twin brother is mentioned. The mention of Perez's brother and the mention of how it was from Tamar that Judah's heirs were produced are clear indications that the reference here is intended to recall the story as it is found in Genesis 38.

Genesis 38 is about how Judah's lineage happened to be continued through Tamar so if we wanted a suitable heading for Genesis 38, the reference in Matt 1:3 could easily function as its heading ("Judah produced Perez and Zerah from Tamar," or, "How Judah produced Perez and Zerah from Tamar"). The reference recalls the story from Genesis 38. Given the story's uniqueness, many readers and hearers would be able to remember the story after hearing it only once.

It pays to notice what it is about the story highlighted in Genesis 38 that early readers and hearers of Matthew would be expected to notice as relevant to the story of the final heir production appearing in Mathew 1. Not all of Genesis 38 parallels Matt 1:18–25 but there is a moment where the two stories converge, producing a whole series of thematic parallels (and some linguistic parallels).

The key parallels occur in the penultimate paragraph but I include here all ten paragraphs of Genesis 38 for context. I have used the Greek version because the linguistic parallels are easier to spot and because the audience of Matthew are listening to Matthew in Greek so the Greek version of Genesis would likely seem to be used by the same audience.

Greek-English Diglot (LXX Gen 38:1-30)

1 Ἐγένετο δὲ ἐν τῷ καιρῷ ἐκείνῳ κατέβη Ιουδας ἀπὸ τῶν ἀδελφῶν αὐτοῦ καὶ ἀφίκετο ἕως πρὸς ἄνθρωπόν τινα Οδολλαμίτην, ᾧ ὄνομα Ιρας. 2 καὶ εἶδεν ἐκεῖ Ιουδας θυγατέρα ἀνθρώπου Χαναναίου, ᾗ ὄνομα Σαυα, καὶ ἔλαβεν αὐτὴν καὶ εἰσῆλθεν πρὸς αὐτήν. 3 καὶ συλλαβοῦσα ἔτεκεν υἱὸν καὶ ἐκάλεσεν τὸ ὄνομα αὐτοῦ Ηρ. 4 καὶ συλλαβοῦσα ἔτι ἔτεκεν υἱὸν καὶ ἐκάλεσεν τὸ ὄνομα αὐτοῦ Αυναν. 5 καὶ προσθεῖσα ἔτι ἔτεκεν υἱὸν καὶ ἐκάλεσεν τὸ ὄνομα αὐτοῦ Σηλωμ. αὐτὴ δὲ ἦν ἐν Χασβι, ἡνίκα ἔτεκεν αὐτούς.

Now it happened at that time that Judah went down from his brothers and arrived as far as a certain Adullamite man, whose name was Hirah. And there Judah saw a Canaanite man's daughter, whose name was Shua. And he took her as wife and he had intercourse with her. She conceived and gave birth to a son and called his name Er. And after she had conceived again, she gave birth to a son and called his name Onan. And further again, she gave birth to a son and she called his name Shelah. And she was in Qasbi when she gave birth to them.

6 καὶ ἔλαβεν Ιουδας γυναῖκα Ηρ τῷ πρωτοτόκῳ αὐτοῦ, ᾗ ὄνομα Θαμαρ. 7 ἐγένετο δὲ Ηρ πρωτότοκος Ιουδα πονηρὸς ἐναντίον κυρίου, καὶ ἀπέκτεινεν αὐτὸν ὁ θεός. 8 εἶπεν δὲ Ιουδας τῷ Αυναν Εἴσελθε πρὸς τὴν γυναῖκα τοῦ ἀδελφοῦ σου καὶ γάμβρευσαι αὐτὴν καὶ ἀνάστησον σπέρμα τῷ ἀδελφῷ σου.

And Judah took for Er his firstborn a wife, her name was Tamar. It happened that Judah's firstborn was wicked in the sight of the Lord and God killed him. Then Judah said to Onan, "Go have intercourse with your brother's wife and be married-as-kin to her and raise offspring for your brother."

9 γνοὺς δὲ Αυναν ὅτι οὐκ αὐτῷ ἔσται τὸ σπέρμα, ἐγίνετο ὅταν εἰσήρχετο πρὸς τὴν γυναῖκα τοῦ ἀδελφοῦ αὐτοῦ, ἐξέχεεν ἐπὶ τὴν γῆν τοῦ μὴ δοῦναι σπέρμα τῷ ἀδελφῷ αὐτοῦ. 10 πονηρὸν δὲ ἐφάνη ἐναντίον τοῦ θεοῦ ὅτι ἐποίησεν τοῦτο, καὶ ἐθανάτωσεν καὶ τοῦτον.

But as Onan knew that the offspring would not be his, he would spill his semen on the ground during intercourse with his brother's wife, so that he would not give offspring to his brother. It was seen to be evil in the sight of God that he did this and God put him to death also.

Greek-English Diglot (LXX Gen 38:1-30)

11 εἶπεν δὲ Ιουδας Θαμαρ τῇ νύμφῃ αὐτοῦ Κάθου χήρα ἐν τῷ οἴκῳ τοῦ πατρός σου, ἕως μέγας γένηται Σηλωμ ὁ υἱός μου· εἶπεν γὰρ Μήποτε ἀποθάνη καὶ οὗτος ὥσπερ οἱ ἀδελφοὶ αὐτοῦ. ἀπελθοῦσα δὲ Θαμαρ ἐκάθητο ἐν τῷ οἴκῳ τοῦ πατρὸς αὐτῆς.

Then Judah said to Tamar, his daughter-in-law, "Go live as a widow in the house of your father. Until my son Shelah is mature." Judah only said this to prevent Shelah's expected death like his brothers. Having departed, Tamar stayed in the house of her father.

12 Ἐπληθύνθησαν δὲ αἱ ἡμέραι καὶ ἀπέθανεν Σαυα ἡ γυνὴ Ιουδα· καὶ παρακληθεὶς Ιουδας ἀνέβη ἐπὶ τοὺς κείροντας τὰ πρόβατα αὐτοῦ, αὐτὸς καὶ Ιρας ὁ ποιμὴν αὐτοῦ ὁ Οδολλαμίτης, εἰς Θαμνα. 13 καὶ ἀπηγγέλη Θαμαρ τῇ νύμφῃ αὐτοῦ λέγοντες Ἰδοὺ ὁ πενθερός σου ἀναβαίνει εἰς Θαμνα κεῖραι τὰ πρόβατα αὐτοῦ.

Time went on, and the wife of Judah, Shua, died. And after Judah had been comforted, he went up to Timnah to those who were shearing his sheep, he and the shepherd of his, Hirah the Adullamite. And this was reported to his daughter-in-law Tamar, "Behold your father-in-law is going up to Timnah to shear his sheep."

14 καὶ περιελομένη τὰ ἱμάτια τῆς χηρεύσεως ἀφ᾽ ἑαυτῆς περιεβάλετο θέριστρον καὶ ἐκαλλωπίσατο καὶ ἐκάθισεν πρὸς ταῖς πύλαις Αιναν, ἥ ἐστιν ἐν παρόδῳ Θαμνα· εἶδεν γὰρ ὅτι μέγας γέγονεν Σηλωμ, αὐτὸς δὲ οὐκ ἔδωκεν αὐτὴν αὐτῷ γυναῖκα.

And taking off the garments of her widowhood. She put on a lightweight garment and adorned her face and sat down near the gates of Ainan, which is on the way past Timnah, for she saw that Shelah was now mature yet Judah still did not give her to him as wife.

Greek-English Diglot (LXX Gen 38:1-30)

15 καὶ ἰδὼν αὐτὴν Ιουδας ἔδοξεν αὐτὴν πόρνην εἶναι· κατεκαλύψατο γὰρ τὸ πρόσωπον αὐτῆς, καὶ οὐκ ἐπέγνω αὐτήν. 16 ἐξέκλινεν δὲ πρὸς αὐτὴν τὴν ὁδὸν καὶ εἶπεν αὐτῇ Ἔασόν με εἰσελθεῖν πρὸς σέ· οὐ γὰρ ἔγνω ὅτι ἡ νύμφη αὐτοῦ ἐστιν. ἡ δὲ εἶπεν Τί μοι δώσεις, ἐὰν εἰσέλθῃς πρός με; 17 ὁ δὲ εἶπεν Ἐγώ σοι ἀποστελῶ ἔριφον αἰγῶν ἐκ τῶν προβάτων. ἡ δὲ εἶπεν Ἐὰν δῷς ἀρραβῶνα ἕως τοῦ ἀποστεῖλαί σε. 18 ὁ δὲ εἶπεν Τίνα τὸν ἀρραβῶνά σοι δώσω; ἡ δὲ εἶπεν Τὸν δακτύλιόν σου καὶ τὸν ὁρμίσκον καὶ τὴν ῥάβδον τὴν ἐν τῇ χειρί σου. καὶ ἔδωκεν αὐτῇ καὶ εἰσῆλθεν πρὸς αὐτήν, καὶ ἐν γαστρὶ ἔλαβεν ἐξ αὐτοῦ. 19 καὶ ἀναστᾶσα ἀπῆλθεν καὶ περιείλατο τὸ θέριστρον ἀφ᾽ ἑαυτῆς καὶ ἐνεδύσατο τὰ ἱμάτια τῆς χηρεύσεως αὐτῆς.

20 ἀπέστειλεν δὲ Ιουδας τὸν ἔριφον ἐξ αἰγῶν ἐν χειρὶ τοῦ ποιμένος αὐτοῦ τοῦ Οδολλαμίτου κομίσασθαι τὸν ἀρραβῶνα παρὰ τῆς γυναικός, καὶ οὐχ εὗρεν αὐτήν. 21 ἐπηρώτησεν δὲ τοὺς ἄνδρας τοὺς ἐκ τοῦ τόπου Ποῦ ἐστιν ἡ πόρνη ἡ γενομένη ἐν Αιναν ἐπὶ τῆς ὁδοῦ; καὶ εἶπαν Οὐκ ἦν ἐνταῦθα πόρνη. 22 καὶ ἀπεστράφη πρὸς Ιουδαν καὶ εἶπεν Οὐχ εὗρον, καὶ οἱ ἄνθρωποι οἱ ἐκ τοῦ τόπου λέγουσιν μὴ εἶναι ὧδε πόρνην. 23 εἶπεν δὲ Ιουδας Ἐχέτω αὐτά, ἀλλὰ μήποτε καταγελασθῶμεν· ἐγὼ μὲν ἀπέσταλκα τὸν ἔριφον τοῦτον, σὺ δὲ οὐχ εὕρηκας.

And when Judah saw her, he thought she was a prostitute for she had disguised her face and he did not recognize her. Then he turned aside to her from the path and said to her, "Allow me to have intercourse with you," since he did not recognize that she was his daughter-in-law. And she said, "What will you give me for having intercourse with me?" And he said, "I will send to you a young goat from the goats from the flocks." And she said, "If you give a pledge until you send it." And he said, "What pledge shall I give to you?" And she said, "Your ring and your neck scarf and the staff that is in your hand." And he gave them to her, and he had intercourse with her, and she gained pregnancy from him. And rising up, she went away, and she took off her light-weight garment, and put on the garments of widowhood.

Now, Judah sent the young goat from the goats by the hand of his shepherd the Adullamite to recover the pledge from the woman and he did not find her. And then he asked the men of the place, "Where is the prostitute who was at Ainan by the road?" And they said, "There was no prostitute here." And he returned to Judah and said, "I did not find. And the people from that place say that there was no prostitute there." And Judah said, "Let her have them. But let us not be laughed at. I've done my part. I've sent this young goat but you have not found."

Greek-English Diglot (LXX Gen 38:1-30)

24 Ἐγένετο δὲ μετὰ τρίμηνον ἀπηγγέλη
τῷ Ιουδα λέγοντες Ἐκπεπόρνευκεν
Θαμαρ ἡ νύμφη σου καὶ ἰδοὺ ἐν γαστρὶ
ἔχει ἐκ πορνείας. εἶπεν δὲ Ιουδας
Ἐξαγάγετε αὐτήν, καὶ κατακαυθήτω.
25 αὐτὴ δὲ ἀγομένη ἀπέστειλεν πρὸς
τὸν πενθερὸν αὐτῆς λέγουσα Ἐκ τοῦ
ἀνθρώπου, τίνος ταῦτά ἐστιν, ἐγὼ ἐν
γαστρὶ ἔχω. καὶ εἶπεν Ἐπίγνωθι, τίνος ὁ
δακτύλιος καὶ ὁ ὁρμίσκος καὶ ἡ ῥάβδος
αὕτη. 26 ἐπέγνω δὲ Ιουδας καὶ εἶπεν
Δεδικαίωται Θαμαρ ἢ ἐγώ, οὗ εἵνεκεν οὐκ
ἔδωκα αὐτὴν Σηλωμ τῷ υἱῷ μου. καὶ οὐ
προσέθετο ἔτι τοῦ γνῶναι αὐτήν.

27 Ἐγένετο δὲ ἡνίκα ἔτικτεν, καὶ τῇδε ἦν
δίδυμα ἐν τῇ γαστρὶ αὐτῆς. 28 ἐγένετο δὲ
ἐν τῷ τίκτειν αὐτὴν ὁ εἷς προεξήνεγκεν
τὴν χεῖρα· λαβοῦσα δὲ ἡ μαῖα ἔδησεν
ἐπὶ τὴν χεῖρα αὐτοῦ κόκκινον λέγουσα
Οὗτος ἐξελεύσεται πρότερος. 29 ὡς
δὲ ἐπισυνήγαγεν τὴν χεῖρα, καὶ εὐθὺς
ἐξῆλθεν ὁ ἀδελφὸς αὐτοῦ. ἡ δὲ εἶπεν Τί
διεκόπη διὰ σὲ φραγμός; καὶ ἐκάλεσεν τὸ
ὄνομα αὐτοῦ Φαρες. 30 καὶ μετὰ τοῦτο
ἐξῆλθεν ὁ ἀδελφὸς αὐτοῦ, ἐφ' ᾧ ἦν ἐπὶ τῇ
χειρὶ αὐτοῦ τὸ κόκκινον· καὶ ἐκάλεσεν τὸ
ὄνομα αὐτοῦ Ζαρα.

Now it happened that after a few
months it was reported to Judah, "Your
daughter-in-law Tamar has prostituted
herself and, behold, she has a pregnancy
from her prostitution." Then Judah said,
"Bring her to be burned." But as she was
being brought, she sent a message to her
father-in-law saying, "I have a pregnancy
from the man whose things these are."
And she said, "Notice whose is the ring
and the scarf and this staff." Then Judah
recognized them and said, "Tamar has
been proven right over me, because I did
not give her to my son Shelah." And he
did not know her again.

Now it happened that at the time when
she gave birth that she had twins in her
belly and it happened during giving
birth that one twin put his hand out and
taking it the midwife bound red material
on his hand saying, "This one will come
out first." But when he retracted his
hand, then immediately out came his
brother, and she said, "What sort of a
barrier has been cut through because of
you?!" And she called his name Perez.
And afterward, his brother came out
who had the red material on his hand,
she called his name Zerah.

When Judah finds out that Tamar is pregnant he makes a decision about
what to do. It is at this point that there is a whole series of correspondences
to observe concerning Matt 1:18–25 when Joseph realizes that Mary is
pregnant and he makes a decision about what to do.

Both stories are similarly set up with a scenario concerning a woman
who is betrothed and before the patriarch has accepted her he finds out
that she is already pregnant. What the man decides he will do is not followed through because his plan is interrupted. The outcome is that he
accepts paternity.

Note six parallels:

1. a betrothed woman is waiting on a man to welcome her into his household;

2. the man discovers the woman is already pregnant;

3. the man presumes a lack of his own paternity;

4. the man makes a decision about what to do;

5. that decision is then overridden by a revelation of new information; and

6. the outcome is that the man gains the offspring as his heir by gaining the status of paternity.

There are even more parallels to notice but it is first worth considering why there are parallels in the first place. What is the significance of having such parallels?

The point of intended similarities between two stories is to highlight the differences within the similarities. Differences can be observed once the similarities are seen. If there were no similarities then it would not be easy to make any comparisons. Once similarities have been drawn, the comparisons can be made. In other words, the similarities draw attention to what is similar so that we can observe what is different within the similarities.

There is contrast to be observed between the two stories by comparing each man's response, which is completely opposite. How Joseph responds to Mary's pregnancy is shown to be in complete contrast to how Judah responds to Tamar's pregnancy.

The differences can be observed in terms of three aspects: firstly, the time taken for each man to respond to the woman's pregnancy; secondly, the private or public nature of the response; and thirdly, how judgmental the man is in relation to the woman.

Firstly, Judah responds quickly. In terms of the amount of time it takes for Judah to respond it is an instant response without Judah taking any time to consider anything. The response is rushed. In contrast, Joseph's response time is at a much slower pace. Joseph realizes Mary is pregnant and considers his options, resolving what he will do and then he goes to sleep before enacting any plan.

Secondly, Judah responds publicly by speaking to others and calling for a public response so that Tamar can be burned in public. In contrast, Joseph resists any kind of publicity, not even wanting Mary to be talked about publicly. Joseph does not get the public involved in his plan to divorce Mary.

Thirdly, Judah stands in judgment over Tamar, demonstrating a judgmental opinion by assuming that she is guilty of *porneia* (πορνεία) and sentencing her to death. In contrast, Joseph displays no judgment of Mary whatsoever. Joseph is mindful of his own actions rather than blaming Mary for anything. Joseph decides to step aside gracefully as though he simply does not think he should be claiming rights to Mary and her child.

The point of the story parallels is to notice how each of these two men respond to the betrothed woman's pregnancy. Judah's response is rushed, rash, public, and judgmental. By contrast, Joseph's response is rather considered, private, discreet, and nonjudgmental (he is critical of his own potential behavior and not critical of Mary).

The cumulative effect of these inverted correspondences between Judah and Joseph is to tell a similar story with contrasting characters. Telling a similar story helps us identify the genre of the story. Each story tells of unplanned paternity. The contrasting characters begin with a similar predicament and end up with a similar outcome whilst each man's response to the respective pregnant woman is contrasted.

By comparing Joseph with Judah, Joseph's inherent refusal to judge Mary is further apparent. Judah's inclination to be judgmental is not depicted as being a right inclination but presented as a self-righteous reaction. Matthew 1 is not suggesting that the righteous response would be for Joseph to have been judgmental like Judah (as if Joseph is avoiding doing the right thing). Rather, Joseph's lack of judgmental attitude toward Mary (and lack of entitlement) is why he is labeled as being righteous/inculpable. According to the contrast with Judah, Joseph's inclination is the opposite of judgmental.

We are invited to notice that the contrast indicates that the idea of a harsh or violent response by the man could be a potential outcome in Joseph's case before we know how he would respond. It might be that the man to whom Mary is betrothed could potentially be going to react violently or jeopardize the well-being of Mary and her child (just as Judah initially did). But the potential for Joseph to response in such a way is immediately mitigated by saying "Joseph, being a righteous man." Any concern that may potentially arise in verse 18 is immediately alleviated at the beginning of verse 19. Any readers and hearers wondering about what kind of man Joseph is at the end of verse 18 are immediately informed in verse 19 that Joseph is not like Judah.

It pays to examine the most interesting parallel in which the newer story quotes a line from the older story, that is, "he did not know her." Just prior to the mention of the birth each story mentions the man's new action according to the negative assertion that he did not know her.

Within Matt 1:18–25, the expression "he did not know her" (οὐκ ἐγίνωσκεν αὐτὴν) is the third reference to a lack of sexual intimacy between Mary and Joseph. The first reference is found in verse 18 ("before they came together") in which the lack of sexual intimacy is expressed as a lack of union, that is, "before they united" (πρὶν ἢ συνελθεῖν αὐτοὺς). The second reference is an indirect reference in verse 19 using the opposite kind of language to pursuing sexual relations, namely Joseph is pursuing separation and avoiding uniting with Mary since "he decided he would quietly divorce her" (ἐβουλήθη λάθρᾳ ἀπολῦσαι αὐτήν). The third reference appears in verse 25 in which the lack of sexual intimacy is mentioned using the language of "not knowing" (οὐκ ἐγίνωσκεν αὐτὴν) quoting a line from the story of Judah and Tamar.

In Matt 1:18–25 there are three references to a lack of sexual relations leave no room for doubt that, within the story, Joseph was never sexually united with Mary. The obvious point is that Mary's child cannot possibly have been Joseph's biological offspring. The first reference to the lack of sexual intimacy (v. 18) identifies both partners as responsible for the lack of union; the second reference (v. 19) identifies it as Joseph's intention not to have a marital relationship with Mary; and the third reference (v. 25) likewise identifies the lack of sexual relations from Joseph's side. The third reference to a lack of sexual intimacy says "he" rather than "they" partly because it is quoting the parallel story in Gen 38:26 in which "he did not know her" was referring to Judah with Tamar. The Greek in Matt 1:25 could even be translated as "he made no attempt to have sex with her," thereby emphasizing Joseph's lack of sexual intentions with Mary as well as keeping his own paternity as divinely granted rather than self-claimed.

The theme of "he did not know her" appears more than once in Genesis 38. In Gen 38:15, when Judah saw Tamar he thought she was a prostitute because she had disguised her face and he did not perceive her real identity. So when Judah had sex with Tamar, the idea is that Judah was "knowing her" unknowingly. So when it finally concludes Judah's role by saying "thereafter he did not know her again" (καὶ οὐ προσέθετο ἔτι τοῦ γνῶναι αὐτήν) it reiterates the same theme of having become a father without knowing by cleverly choosing to highlight the theme of not knowing operating throughout the whole story.

In Judah's case it refers to it being from that time onward (after the story episode). In Joseph's case it refers to the time before Mary gave birth (up until the end of the story episode). For Judah it means that now that he knows that it was Tamar that he had inadvertently "known" he will never again know her. There is a shift happening for Judah on more than one level including the level of known paternity, the level of sexual intimacy, and at the level of intention.

For Joseph it is not depicting a shift of intention or of sexual intimacy but a consistency in the kind of "not knowing" of Mary. Throughout Matt 1:18–25 Joseph is consistently (three times) presented as not knowing Mary at three potential moments.

The most significant shift for Judah is that he begins to behave rightly. Judah gets his act together and begins to take responsibility for his own actions, not doing whatever he wants to do or making others do what he commands. It shows the maturing of Judah into someone more respectable. Judah has suddenly recognized that he was not inculpable for the way he had been treating Tamar. It is a repentant moment for Judah who implicates himself as being not in the right by declaring that it is Tamar, after all, who is innocent not Judah himself: "It is she who is not guilty rather than me" (Δεδικαίωται Θαμαρ ἢ ἐγώ). After that, "he did not know her again" (οὐ προσέθετο ἔτι τοῦ γνῶναι αὐτήν).

In Joseph's case, Joseph has already been behaving righteously/innocently throughout the story episode. It is at this point that the two stories converge linguistically: in Judah's case he does not know her (Tamar) again; in Joseph's case he does not know her (Mary) still.

Actually, in Judah's case too his not knowing still continues, albeit in a different way. Judah did not truly perceive Tamar earlier on so when it says "thereafter he did not know her again" it could also be read as though saying he *continued* not to know her. In Judah's case he had continually misperceived who Tamar really was until Tamar eventually takes advantage of the misperception so as to be misperceived deliberately in order to be able to get the child she has been promised more than once. Judah had blocked his lineage from continuing because he had wrongly perceived Tamar to be guilty for the death of her first two husbands (his first two sons) and he thought she was not loyal to his lineage but Tamar proved otherwise by rectifying things without Judah knowing. When finally Judah knows he still does not *know* her since he did not earlier *know* her to be Tamar and now he *knows* not to *know* her anymore. Here, the not knowing is not only literal knowing (sexual) it also picks up on the idea of (mis)perception of who Tamar really is—she is carrying his offspring and his legacy should continue from her (she had, in fact, always been faithful to his family). It is a cleverly constructed scene of Judah making a critical discovery which Aristotle would have identified to be ἀναγνώρισις ("recognition," "realization") defined as "shifting from ignorance to knowledge" ("ἐξ ἀγνοίας εἰς γνῶσιν μεταβολή").[1]

Matt 1:18–25 utilizes a similar kind of "recognition" scene by having Joseph come to realize that Mary is carrying the heir (his lineage is continuing, unexpectedly, from her). He recognizes his own surprise paternity by divine authority. Joseph's initial plan to divorce Mary quietly was based on his not knowing Mary (sexually) and ignorance of his own future status of paternity. He initially only knows that the child is not his to claim when he is suddenly endowed with a parental role. After his fatherhood is divinely conferred, the story again mentions that Joseph still does not know Mary by quoting the parallel story of Judah's intentions of "not knowing." Joseph's status as parent and husband has no basis in carnal knowledge of Mary so the only real change for Joseph is that his parental status is solely reliant on being divinely sanctioned.

How Judah became the father of Perez and Zerah and how Joseph ended up being known as Jesus's father are parallel stories of heirs produced without the fathers "knowing" the mothers of the heirs. Judah did not know Tamar and Joseph did not know Mary. Each man is surprised to discover that the pregnant woman is continuing his lineage.

Conclusion

Joseph did not "know" Mary in the making of the heir and Joseph was surprised to "know" it should be his child. It is portrayed as less of a mystery to the readers and hearers of the story but it is left relatively under-explained and mysterious for Joseph within the story—the two reasons given to Joseph are supernatural, transcending human knowledge ("the heir in her is from the Holy Spirit" τὸ γὰρ ἐν αὐτῇ γεννηθὲν ἐκ πνεύματός ἐστιν ἁγίου) and prophetic ("he will save his people from their sins" (αὐτὸς γὰρ σώσει τὸν λαὸν αὐτοῦ ἀπὸ τῶν ἁμαρτιῶν αὐτῶν). Joseph

1. Aristotle, *Poetics*, 1452a30.

cooperates without fully comprehending. He does not really know how Mary is carrying within her the future Messiah.

It is now clear why Matt 1:18–25 focused on Joseph's intentions. The story parallels the story of Judah in Genesis 38 by highlighting the theme of not knowing and by highlighting the inverted responses of Judah and Joseph to the betrothed women. Judah's culpable behavior had to be intercepted in order for him to stop preventing his lineage continuing from Tamar. Joseph's righteous behavior had to be intercepted in order for him to stop preventing the necessary lineage continuing from Mary. Thus Joseph's initial response to avoid taking in the pregnant Mary parallels and inverts Judah's initial response to avoid taking in the pregnant Tamar. Judah is motivated to publicly and disdainfully reject the woman carrying the potential heir. Joseph is motivated to privately and respectfully reject the woman carrying the potential heir.

Joseph's intentions are presented as being ignorant of the future and lacking divine permission to claim Mary and her child. Joseph does not initially know that the child Mary is carrying should be known as his own heir. Joseph's paternity, like Judah's paternity, comes as a surprise. By comparing the story parallel mentioned in Matt 1:3, the genre is clarified to be a scene in which the paternity is acknowledged as a surprise revelation. Not only is it a surprise to the patriarch himself it is a surprising story being linked with another surprising story for the readers and hearers of Matthew 1.

It is now becoming clear that how the final heir was produced is not, after all, unlike all the previous heirs, at least not unlike how Judah's lineage continued from Tamar which contains several points of correspondence and which is why Genesis 38 is referenced in Matthew 1 and a portion of Judah's and Tamar's story is quoted in verse 25.

Surely, these parallels are enough. Why have three more stories? Why have the references to how Salmon produced Boaz *from Rahab*, how Boaz produced Obed *from Ruth*, and how David produced Solomon *from her of Uriah*? That is our final question for Matthew 1.

The Pattern of the Five References to Mothers

Overview

This chapter looks at the overall pattern of the five references to mothers in Matthew 1. Like the first reference, the second, third, and fourth references also fit the overall pattern of highlighting the theme of unplanned paternity. In the second reference (v. 5), the narrator reveals the father of Rahab's child from a story originally about a named woman (Rahab) with two unnamed men whilst leaving the woman unnamed in the fourth reference as a story of two named men and an unnamed woman (Bathsheba). The center story of how Boaz became known as the father of Ruth's son (Obed) has the most in common with how Joseph became known as the father of Mary's son (Jesus) with the difference being that Boaz never knew he would be known as the child's father. The concentric pattern of five highlighted cases of surprise paternity dovetails with the pattern of divine providence in which the divine agenda is accomplished when the human patriarchal prerogative is absent.

THE REFERENCES TO HEIRS produced "from Rahab," "from Ruth," and "from her of Uriah" (Bathsheba) might seem unnecessary given that the first and fifth references to the stories of heirs produced "from Tamar" and "from Mary" correspond with so many parallels.

The overall pattern of five stories forms a concentric (or "chiastic") structure in which the first highlighted story (Judah's heir-production from Tamar) has correspondences with the fifth highlighted story (Joseph's heir-production from Mary). The second and fourth stories are meant to correspond in some way (Salmon's heir-production from Rahab; David's heir-production from Uriah's wife), leaving the center story as the center of the structure (Boaz's heir-production from Ruth). Perhaps the best way to introduce the three remaining cases is to begin with the fourth case.

The fourth reference highlighting how David produced his heir ("David produced Solomon from her of Uriah") appears in verse 6. The reference suggests that David produced an heir adulterously from another man's wife. In the original story found in 2 Samuel 11, after David illicitly takes Uriah's wife, David tries to make Uriah think Uriah himself is the father of the pregnancy and when that fails David organizes for Uriah to be killed in battle. Both sins (adultery and murder) are presented in 2 Samuel as being committed by David against Uriah.

In Matthew 1, the reference to David producing his heir from "her of Uriah" collapses three originally separate story episodes about David together and presents it as a single story. The effect is that David's flaws are on display. It makes David look even more irrational and flawed than when reading the original story episodes. By saying that Solomon was produced "from Uriah's wife" it is presented as though the child David produced was produced illicitly from another man's wife even though, according to the original story (in 2 Sam 12:13–25), Solomon was the second child David produced from Bathsheba only *after* Bathsheba became one of David's legal wives. Also, the succession of Solomon only eventuates because Bathsheba and Nathan conspire to make it happen but this is not part of the story in 2 Samuel (it is only found in 1 Kings).

Lest we think that collapsing the three story episodes into one is merely a side-effect of wanting to simplify things for the genealogical account in Matt 1:2–16, there is an unnecessary complication. That is, rather than naming Bathsheba as the mother in verse 6, it complicates things by referring to her indirectly as "her of Uriah" even though in the four other references to mothers in the genealogy the mothers are named.

David's sins against Uriah would still have been obvious had Matt 1:6 said, "David produced Solomon from Uriah's Bathsheba." But leaving Bathsheba unnamed requires an explanation.

The explanation can be found by comparing the second highlighted case to how an heir was produced, namely how "Salmon produced Boaz from Rahab." How Salmon produced Boaz from Rahab is similarly complicated when trying to match it up with an earlier story in the scriptures due to the absence of any mention of Salmon getting together with Rahab to produce children. The scriptures only contain a story about Rahab (in Joshua

2) and seemingly no story about Salmon. How are we expected to map this reference to Salmon and Rahab onto the story in Joshua 2?

It seems that Salmon's absence from Rahab's story in Joshua 2 can be explained as absence in name only. According to the reference in Matt 1:5, we might find Salmon in Rahab's story if we look for Salmon's presence within that story. Salmon might be seen to be one of the two unnamed men in Rahab's story. Two unnamed "spies" visit Rahab's house and stay the night. As son of Nashon, a high ranking military man, Salmon might be read into Rahab's story as one of the unnamed spies who stayed the night at Rahab's house. Matt 1:5 seems to be expecting us to read Salmon into Rahab's story when it says, "Salmon produced Boaz from Rahab."

Note the resulting correspondence here with how the fourth highlighted heir production is presented in Matt 1:6. Rahab's story (referenced in verse 5) was originally a story of a woman and two unnamed men. In the fourth case referenced (in verse 6) a story is presented of two named men and an unnamed woman (Bathsheba). Just as we can be expected to name the unnamed mother (Bathsheba), we can now be expected to know the name of the unnamed father (Salmon) in Rahab's story. The two stories are counterbalanced as they are presented in Matthew by naming the unnamed father (second highlighted case) and not naming the named mother (fourth highlighted case).

There are further correlations to observe between the two stories. One story concerns David "seeing" Bathsheba and the other story of Rahab "hiding" the two spies. Also, both stories concern a woman and a roof. David sees Bathsheba when he is on his roof; Rahab hides the two men from being seen on her roof. Another correspondence is that there is a moment in both stories in which the respective woman outwits a king by convincing the king to believe something different. We might not have noticed these correlations had they not been linked together in Matt 1:5 and Matt 1:6 as the second and fourth highlighted cases of heirs produced.

A significant feature in the second and fourth highlighted references to heirs produced is the element of surprise paternity. How Salmon is known to be the father of Boaz is a surprise to us. We did not know that Salmon was the father of Boaz until it was revealed in Matthew 1. This may also have been a surprise to Salmon himself, to know that Rahab would be carrying his future heir (or perhaps even to be named in Rahab's story). If we could interview the young teenage Salmon before he is ready to marry and enquire as to his future plans to have children he is unlikely to predict that his progeny will be produced from Rahab (a Canaanite sex worker from Jericho). Also, if we were to consider all of the potential fathers who might possibly have been the father of Rahab's child there are many potential fathers making it difficult to know who the father of Rahab's child might be. Matthew 1 reveals the father of Rahab's child as another case of surprising unplanned paternity.

Surprise paternity is also a feature of the fourth reference, namely David's heir Solomon being produced from another man's wife. The unusual way it is said in Matt 1:6 highlights the element of surprise (from another man's wife). Also, within the original story, Bathsheba's announcement to David in 2 Sam 11:5 ("I am pregnant") is presented as an unplanned pregnancy.

The oversimplified reference to David producing Solomon "from Uriah's wife" in Matt 1:6 also highlights the surprise outcome since the story in 2 Samuel does not present David taking Uriah's wife Bathsheba in order to produce an heir. David is not planning to produce the next king by taking another man's wife. Also, according to 1 Kings, David is not particularly interested in making Solomon his heir. By referencing the entire saga simply as "David produced Solomon from her of Uriah," it effectively highlights that how David became the father of his heir happened inadvertently, without him planning it out that way. Matt 1:6 presupposes the production of Solomon as being an unplanned heir.

The theme of "unplanned heir production" can also be seen in the third highlighted reference to how a progenitor acquired an heir, that is, how Boaz produced Obed from Ruth. Boaz's paternity is expressly presented as contrary to what Boaz was planning. He was not planning to raise his own child from Ruth. Instead, he generously anticipated raising offspring for Ruth's first husband, Mahlon, in the lineage of Elimelech. Despite this plan, at the end of the book of Ruth, the child Obed appears, surprisingly, in Boaz's lineage.

Apparently, not one of the five patriarchal progenitors in these five stories of how their heirs were produced was planning it to turn out that way. The pattern highlights a missing prerogative in each of the five cases for the human patriarch as though the Messiah's coming is accomplished in the absence of these patriarch's making it happen. It pays to unpack the third case which is the most detailed.

The third highlighted reference to how a particular progenitor gained an heir ("Boaz produced Obed from Ruth") is not only structurally central but it is also the central point, that is, it explains the entire pattern of five by clarifying how the Messiah is the product of his lineage.

The story of how Boaz produced Obed from Ruth refers to a self-contained story with its own book (making it easier to study the story). In the book of Ruth we can observe important themes which reappear in the story of how Joseph's heir Jesus was produced from Mary in Matt 1:18–25.

Both stories are connected to their own genealogies. After the story of how Ruth and Boaz meet, marry, and have a child there follows a genealogy that initially seems not to fit the story. Similarly, the Matthean genealogy attached to the beginning of the story of Jesus being born to Mary and Joseph initially seems ill-fitting since it might not seem to be giving Jesus's genealogy. The more we can understand how the one genealogy fits its story the more it helps with understanding how the other fits with its attached story since how the genealogy before Matt 1:18–25 works with the story presents a similar problem to how the genealogy after Ruth 4:17 works.

In both Matthew and Ruth the lineages are not what we might have expected. In Matthew, the lineage consists of Joseph's biological ancestors, not Jesus's. In Ruth, the lineage consists of Boaz's biological ancestors, not Mahlon's (Ruth's first husband). In Matthew, Joseph does not intend to assume paternity of a child that is not his. In the book of Ruth, Boaz does not intend to assume paternity of a child that should not be counted as his (but should be counted as Mahlon's in the line of Elimelech). Both of these patriarchs ultimately gain paternity which they did not plan to gain. Both men had planned something less self-serving. In both cases, paternity is gained because of divine providential intervention. Apparently, it is *because* Boaz is *not* planning to make the child his own heir that the genealogy in Ruth 4:18–22 proclaims Boaz as the father. This is the same pattern operating in the case of Joseph. The difference is that Boaz may never have known the end of the story whereas Joseph is told the ending of the story in which he will be known as the father of the child.

The parallels between Boaz and Joseph are instructive. In the book of Ruth, Boaz is introduced in Ruth 2 in a positive way, as a wealthy and generous relative of Ruth's mother-in-law Naomi (Ruth 2:1) and he is able to provide not only sustenance for Ruth's gleaning (Ruth 2:8) but he shows real concern for Ruth and Naomi's wellbeing (Ruth 2:9–13). He makes sure that no workers would harass Ruth (Ruth 2:8b–9); he makes sure she has a place to eat at the mealtime (Ruth 2:14); he makes sure the workers leave plenty of sheaves for her to glean (Ruth 2: 15–16); but he is not pursuing Ruth for himself.

In other words, Boaz is presented with a lack of self-interest. He has the power to take things for himself. He has the power to make things happen. But he does not use his strength for his own agenda. It seems no coincidence that his name is "Boaz" ("his strength" or "strength is in him") as the story hinges on the potential for action yet he plays a supportive role to the more active women, Naomi and Ruth. How Boaz does (and does not) use his power is key. Boaz is depicted as a man who is only using his power to assist Ruth whilst making no advances on Ruth for himself.

Likewise, in Matthew 1, Joseph is presented as a man who intends to assist Mary's situation by keeping his nonpaternity a secret and he makes no advances or claims on Mary. Neither man takes advantage of the woman. Boaz does not pursue Ruth. Joseph does not pursue Mary. Both men are presented, atypically, as doing the right thing by not asserting any privileges to the women.

With Naomi's encouragement Ruth pursues Boaz. Ruth is the one who proposes marriage; it was not Boaz's idea. Similarly, it was not Joseph's idea to take the pregnant Mary as his wife; it was a divinely given instruction.

Perhaps the most notable parallel between Joseph and Boaz occurs at the scene taking place in the middle of the night at the threshing floor when Boaz suddenly wakes up realizing that a woman is lying next to him. The story again depicts Boaz acting in a supporting role for Ruth. Boaz is exemplary because of his ability to see how impressive Ruth is and for being willing to play a supporting role. Unlike other men during his time he is not pursuing whatever seems good for himself. This is unlike others during that time in which "every man looked out only for his own interests" (Judg 17:6; 21:25). By contrast, Boaz is atypical and is able to perceive and support others' interests rather than feeling entitled to have things play out to his own advantage.

Similarly, Joseph is presented in Matt 1:18–25 as exemplary by not taking Mary when he finds himself in a position to claim her for himself and claim paternity of a child that he is not entitled to call his.

Boaz, rightly, does not want anyone to know that Ruth was laying beside him overnight so he considers the best time for her to avoid being noticed when she leaves (Ruth 3:13). He does not want public rumors starting about Ruth's seemingly lack of sexual restraint. In other words, he is not willing to bring any shame to Ruth.

Similarly, Joseph is, rightly, not willing to cause any shame to Mary so he avoids telling others that Mary's pregnancy is not his. In both cases, the public are not privy to volatile knowledge concerning the woman's seeming sexual activity.

Boaz might easily have taken advantage of his position by having sex with Ruth when the opportunity was presented but he, like Ruth, is thinking beyond his own self-interests. Likewise, Joseph could easily have pursued sexual relations with Mary when it looked like she was already carrying his child; he could potentially have taken Mary as though she was his wife to take. Instead, he knew that it would not be right to assert a marital relationship that was not his to assert nor would it be right to override the child's natural paternity by selfishly asserting his own.

The pattern of five works concentrically. If we had not noticed that how Boaz became the father of Obed from Ruth is the central story in the five highlighted stories of how particular heirs were produced we might have found it difficult to understand Joseph's reticence to take Mary in Matt 1:19–20. As the center of the five highlighted cases, Boaz's exemplary intentions not to produce his own heir affords the most similarities with Joseph's case.

In this way, the pattern of the five cases highlights the absence of, or demotion of, patriarchal prerogative to produce these particular heirs which is apparently what allows the messianic lineage to progress. It is what the patriarchs do *not* control that enables them to acquire their respective heirs.

The whole chapter is intentionally patriarchal in order to lead up to a story about the man who became known as Jesus's father, Joseph, who could potentially boast of coming from a Davidic lineage and could then potentially boast to have acquired the Messiah as his son. Surely Joseph was not so presumptuous as to think he deserved to possess such a prestigious role in the story? What kind of man was it who acquired Jesus as his heir?

Matthew 1 contains the answer to this question. Yes, Joseph was privileged to be known as Jesus's father, having such prestigious paternity. No, Joseph's case involved an unexpected granting of an heir like in Boaz's case in which the patriarch would *not* naturally have claimed the woman and her child for his own lineage.

Joseph, being inculpable, has no desire to disclaim Mary in public or to claim Mary and her child for himself. In this situation, there is space for divine providence to gently sanction such an heir, since there is here, as in Boaz's case, an absence of patriarchal prerogative getting in the way of the divine will.

To simplify, the overall plan in Matthew 1 presents the kind of lineage that produced the Messiah according to two major patterns. The three groups of fourteen generations indicate providential planning beyond the planning of human fathers. Simultaneously, the providential pattern also operates in the five cases in which the patriarchs did not plan the heirs. The two patterns dovetail perfectly because they are both making the same anti-patriarchal point. The double pattern reveals the lack of patriarchal prerogative at work in producing the Messiah by promoting a providential theme as the inverse of the patriarchal prerogative.

There is also complexity within the pattern of three groups of fourteen generations (the outcome of Abraham is kingship; the outcome of kingship is exile; the outcome of exile is the Messiah). There is variety in the notable ethical points concerning the way that the five highlighted patriarchs acquired heirs since the five cases of unplanned paternities are not all exactly the same. Nevertheless, the first, third, and fifth highlighted cases share striking connections in terms of parallels and inverted parallels. Thus it was not Judah's plan for Tamar to continue his lineage—it was planned out by Tamar and God blessed the plan. It was not Boaz's plan to marry Ruth and raise his own offspring from her—the marriage was planned out by Naomi and Ruth and God blessed the plan. It was not Joseph's plan to take the pregnant Mary as his wife—it was an angel's idea sanctioned by scripture and by the Holy Spirit.

Matthew 1 is intentionally patriarchal in order to critique the typical pattern of patriarchs purposefully determining their heirs. The critique within the text operates not by shifting the focus away from the patriarchal figures but by focusing on their lack of patriarchal prerogative to acquire the specific heirs in question. In order to highlight how particular heirs resulted, the references to mothers introduce triangles of relationships into the messianic genealogy. Furthermore, they imply various ambivalences concerning paternity (see figure 5 in which the ambivalent paternities are indicated with dotted lines; for example, note that besides Ruth's first husband, Mahlon, there is also the nameless "somebody" who reneged on the opportunity to marry Ruth).

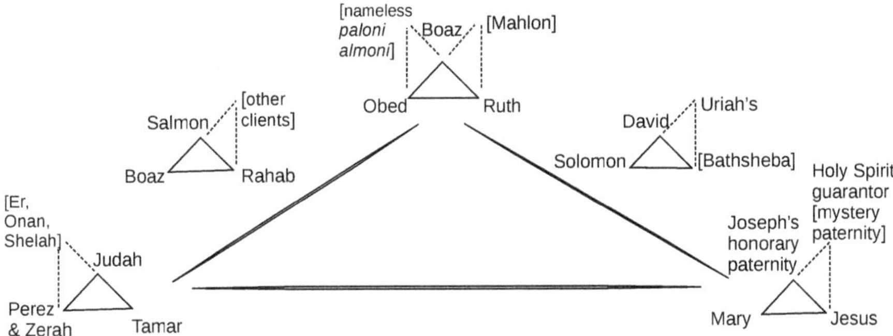

Figure 5. Triangles of relationships and unforeseen paternities.

The portraits of Boaz and Joseph present key examples of a reversal of what Tim Mackie would call a "temptation pattern."[1] A temptation pattern presents characters "seeing" something to benefit themselves and who just "take" without any concern for consequences which, inevitably leads to negative ramifications for themselves and others. In Matthew, this is the pattern that is being undone.

So Boaz "sees" Ruth lying beside him but he does not see this as an opportunity to help himself and so he does not immediately just "take" but stops to consider the larger picture and who might be affected. Joseph "sees" Mary pregnant but he does not see this as an opportunity either to justify himself at Mary's expense or to avail himself of an illegitimate heir and so he does not immediately just "take." Both Boaz and Joseph arise from sleep with a plan that is not simply of their own making or for their own self aggrandizement. Neither Boaz nor Joseph takes advantage of their own privileged position to create a name for themselves or to further their own agendas. This is why their names are raised up in these stories.

Boaz is presented as resisting such a pattern, ultimately enabling a shift from the period of the Judges where the typical man seeks only his own advantage into the period of kingship in which there is a king for the people who will look out for everyone, rather than simply for himself. Joseph is presented as resisting the same temptation pattern, thereby enabling the final messianic heir to arrive—an ideal leader who will look out for his people rather than his own self-advancement.

1. Mackie and Collins, "Design Patterns in the Bible," 1:00–2:55.

It is not purely a patriarchal temptation to "see and take" but it is something that patriarchs are particularly prone to because of their access to greater privilege and power (as well displayed by Judah's early career in Genesis 38).

The pattern in Matthew 1 is intended to highlight the redressing of sins that are depicted as patriarchal. This means that Amy Richter's idea was generally correct insofar as the pattern is meant to be a *redemptive* pattern relating to *sins* and Anne Clements's conclusion is also correct that the pattern *subverts* a *patriarchal* pattern.

The fact that Matthew 1 focuses on the figure of Joseph is no accident of writing. Joseph's situation is presented as a patriarchal dilemma (the potential for a man in Joseph's situation to disgrace Mary or assume to pose as her child's father and take Mary illegitimately).

Scholars have already sensed this solution in varying degrees but have not previously been able to articulate how the pattern works. Some have assumed that the final heir must have arrived in an unprecedented way. Some have seen that the usual pattern of production was already broken somehow in the previous four highlighted cases. So, until now, the idea that there might be a critique of patriarchy operating from within the text has not previously been demonstrated.

Elaine Wainwright has argued that the references to mothers could be seen as a counter-theme within the prevailing patriarchal structure which critiques that structure.[2] Wainwright is even more correct than her proposal suggested. The critique is not only something from outside the text made by resistant readers who choose to expose and critique the patriarchal assumptions in the text. The poetics of Matthew 1 reveals a critique already present *within* the text. The pattern of five references to how five fathers acquired heirs from five mothers present an intentionally anti-patriarchal theme to be seen not only for those of us resisting the text but even for those of reading *with* the text.

Intriguingly, the nine quotations I mentioned at the end of chapter 3 ("The Messianic Lineage in Matt 1:2–16") seemed to suggest that the pattern of unexpected/unplanned paternity had previously been observed by scholars who thought to compare the highlighted fathers. In particular, the final two quotations (by Amy-Jill Levine and by Ruth Kara-Ivanov Kaniel) seemed already to have noted the pattern. Back in chapter 3, I only commented on the amazing impression that the pattern of comparing the

2. Wainwright, *Towards a Feminist Critical Reading*, 172–74.

five paternities seemed already to be understood by others. I now return to comment briefly on each of the nine quotes.

In the first quotation from Hedda Klip, the references to mothers suggest cases in which each of the women are connected to more than one man. The above diagram (triangles of relationships and unforeseen paternities) includes dotted lines to show the connections between the mothers and those who are, surprisingly, "not the fathers." In every case we find an unpredictable tension of who might be revealed to be the father of the heir.

The second quote by Elaine Wainwright suggests that the construction of a patriarchal figure is deconstructed by the intertextual references. Indeed, this is not just a serendipitous side effect but a sign of intentional deconstruction. The references are there to help us see that the typical patriarchal assumptions are meant to be deconstructed. The idea that the men are the principal protagonists securing their own futures is precisely what is being critiqued within Matthew 1, as noted in the third quote by Wim Weren. What might initially have looked like a promotion of patriarchal interests in Matthew 1 (fathers appear as the producers of the heirs) is the very point being critiqued by the text.

The fourth quotation, from Sébastien Doane, observes that the genealogy points out flaws in the highlighted men and subverts ancient hegemonic constructions of masculinity. Indeed, this is not an accidental feature of Matthew 1 since how the highlighted fathers became the fathers of particular heirs undermines the typical patriarchal privilege of making and determining heirs.

The fifth quotation, by F. Scott Spencer, sees that Joseph seems more attuned to his immediate context compared to the first four patriarchal figures, who might appear relatively (and comically) inflexible by contrast to Joseph's more considered actions—behavior that seems not typically "masculine."

In the sixth quote, Jane Schaberg insightfully observes how the men treat the respective women whereby volatile information about sexual conduct is either made public or kept discreet. In the seventh quotation, Christopher Naseri-Mutiti Naseri makes a similar observation by comparing the respective attitudes and intentions of each of the fathers.

In the eighth quotation, Amy-Jill Levine seems already to have successfully detected the theme of unplanned heir production for all five fathers who she refers to as the "undesiring sires" whose "sexual prowess" is challenged. She also observes the undermining of the patriarchal concern for procreation within wedlock which could also be read as promoting celibacy. Indeed, the compound verb used for Joseph "to take along" Mary (in Matt 1:20, 24) would support the idea of a nonsexual marital union.

The ninth quote, from Ruth Kara-Ivanov Kaniel, astutely observes that there is, in fact, biblical language to explain this pattern, namely the fathers are, in some way, described as "unknowing." For example, Boaz awoke, in the dark, and was never able to see Ruth clearly since she left while it was still too dark to see ("she got up before any man could recognize another" Ruth 3:14).[3] Indeed, none of the five patriarchs are in control of knowing what will happen—all five are "in the dark," not knowing in advance how their paternities would be revealed according to Matthew 1.

In combination, the nine quotes cover almost every aspect of the pattern of five heir productions in which the focus is on comparing the intentions and behaviors of five patriarchs within their stories of heir production in order to understand the pattern of their acquired paternities and lack of patriarchal prerogative in determining their heirs.

In conclusion, the opening chapter of the New Testament highlights a concentric pattern of five unplanned paternities in which the focus is on the fathers and their intentions. According to Matthew 1, it is the notable lack of the patriarchal prerogative that brings the final heir, the Messiah, who comes to save his people from their "patriarchal" sins.

---

3. For a more detailed look at the language of knowing ("recognition") in the book of Ruth see Adelman, "Seduction and Recognition, 95–99.

Epilogue

ALTHOUGH THE PRIMARY PURPOSE of this book has been to focus on Matthew 1, there are many questions that remain concerning how the resulting interpretation may affect the way we read the remaining chapters of Matthew. Further research could explore how Matthew might be read in light of the patterns seen in Matthew 1.[1] Here are a few examples to consider.

Jesus's lineage, as given in Matthew 1, is never claimed by Jesus. Such an absence might be intended to show that Jesus did not claim an elite pedigree for himself (or any pedigree other than being "the son of humankind" ὁ υἱὸς τοῦ ἀνθρώπου). Perhaps Jesus is presented in Matthew to be like Joseph by not being the kind of man to claim what he could potentially have claimed for himself.

In Matthew 2, the magi come to honor the infant Jesus as if he were the new king over Judea not because they know his genealogy but because they perceived his destiny written in the heavens. Jesus's future status has been determined by heavenly means rather than according to a biological lineage.

In Matt 3:7–10, John the Baptist is presented as predicting an impending devastation. The Sadducees and Pharisees are presented as being self-assured of their position presuming John should validate their continued status. "Abraham" as "father" suggests a covenantal heritage

---

1. Anderson and Moore note, "Matt 1–2 simultaneously upholds and undercuts traditional valuations of literal fatherhood and patriarchal propagation. In a real sense, this sets the scene for all that follows in the narrative . . . This demotion of literal kinship—not only that between fathers and sons but of other familial relations as well—can be traced from the beginning of the Matthean narrative right through to its conclusion." Anderson and Moore, "Matthew and Masculinity," 75–77.

of security and blessing. To presume such a heritage as inherited status is critiqued in Matt 3:7–10 by John the Baptist who says that God can simply raise up children for Abraham from stones. Again, this continues the theme from Matthew 1, namely that it is not biological paternity that produces God's heirs as well as the idea that leadership is not self-made nor humanly-made but God-made.

At Jesus's baptism (Matt 3:13–17), John the Baptist seems to have figured out that Jesus is the one the people have been waiting for (to lead them with the Holy Spirit and fire) but the moment of public recognition seems to be lost on everyone else. The heavenly dove and voice are not noticed by anyone but Jesus—these are narrated for the benefit of the readers and hearers of the story to provide the revealed knowledge. The heavenly proclamation of Jesus's status is for the audience to know what was not initially publicly perceptible. This continues the same idea as seen in Matt 1:18–25 in which the revealed knowledge differed from what was public knowledge. The story is for the benefit of the audience so as to reveal what was not previously known.

Matthew 5–7 presents the immediate audience of Jesus as a group of men specifically chosen by Jesus to be taught by him. The message Jesus gives these men makes more sense when we understand Jesus's target audience. These men do not have disabilities, or diseases, nor are they slaves. They are free, able-bodied men who Jesus has encouraged to give up patriarchal privileges for the sake of serving God and being taught by Jesus about how the heavenly kingdom operates (in other words to give up their status so as to become servants in the greater heavenly kingdom). Apparently, there is also a wider audience of crowds who also follow Jesus up the mountain to hear Jesus teach. But the patriarchal issues being addressed are particularly suited to the immediate target audience of men that Jesus has chosen to teach.

The first pieces of ethical instruction that Jesus gives his men is that anger, if it is not immediately addressed, is as bad as murder and, similarly, that looking lustfully at other women is as bad as adultery. Jesus's ethics would mean preventing murder and adultery before things escalate into more regrettable things. In Matthew, murder and adultery are presented as patriarchal sins. Anger toward a brother and lusting after another man's wife are presumed to be relevant issues for Jesus to address to his immediate audience. The wider audience also benefits if the patriarchal men learn to avoid murder and adultery since society is better off with less murder and less adultery.

In both cases, Jesus is depicted as extending Moses's teachings (the Ten Commandments had also been directed to men) with stricter teachings to assist in the upholding of the original teachings. The idea is known as "building a fence around the teaching" (or "building a fence around the Torah") since the teachings of Moses are considered so important for the people that more stringent ethics would assist in preserving the older Mosaic ethics. We could say that this is one of the ways that Jesus is presented in Matthew as "saving his people from their sins" (Matt 1:21). The first two sins specifically targeted are clearly presented as patriarchal sins. Perhaps it is no coincidence that these two ethical teachings are also the two ethical topics first hinted at in Matt 1:6 (David's sins against Uriah).

In Matthew 6, Jesus teaches men about not doing their deeds of righteousness publicly but privately (Matt 6:1–6). Again, this continues a theme from Matt 1:18–25 in which Joseph is depicted as inclined to do the right thing by doing it privately as though the two ideas go hand in hand.

In Matthew 13, Jesus expresses how appalled he is by scribes and Pharisees claiming public honor for themselves. Jesus instructs his men to do the opposite, namely not to claim honorable titles for themselves, not to claim the best seats in the synagogue nor to seek public recognition since the greatest men, according to the greatest kingdom, are servants rather than those who seek to be served (Matt 23:1–12). The logic appears to be that a man who claims public honor for himself clashes with what belongs to the divine patriarch. The typical arrogation of patriarchs, patriarchy, and patriarchal agendas conflicts with the divine head of the greater heavenly economy, since there is already a figure-head in the kingdom of the heavens according to Matt 23:9, "And do not call any man your father on earth, for one is your heavenly Father" (καὶ πατέρα μὴ καλέσητε ὑμῶν ἐπὶ τῆς γῆς, εἷς γάρ ἐστιν ὑμῶν ὁ πατὴρ ὁ οὐράνιος). This continues an idea from Matthew 1 in which human patriarchal prerogatives and agendas conflict with the divine will.

In Matt 19:16–30, Jesus is presented as telling the twelve men that just as they have given up patriarchal privileges (rights over properties, households, and families) these will be replaced with a similar yet greater heavenly honor, namely the honor of sitting on thrones overseeing the twelve tribes of Israel at the time of the "re-genesis" or regeneration (παλιγγενεσία). Whether the twelve men literally or figuratively receive such an honor is not clear. What is clear is that the relinquishment of earthly privileges is encouraged. Household honor is not considered to be a complete loss since it returns in greater form and measure once divested from the ordinary realm and invested in the heavenly realm or heavenly economy.

In Matthew 26, Jesus finds his own mission difficult to do. Jesus's own will would be not to go to Jerusalem to face death but he believes that it is what needs to be done according to his heavenly father's will (πλὴν οὐχ ὡς ἐγὼ θέλω ἀλλ' ὡς σύ). Even Jesus does not pursue his own personal will in Matthew.

In Matthew 28, a somewhat genealogical context returns in order to correspond to an element in Matthew 1 not discussed above. The expression "and his brothers" appears twice in Matthew 1 in the first and second groups of ancestry (Matt 1:2, 11). Other than these two references, the genealogy in Matthew 1 is strictly lineal. The expression hints at other potential horizontal lineages branching out from the said heirs. It indicates that there are two points in the ancestry where we might potentially think about other genealogical branches branching out.

In Matt 1:2 it says, "Jacob produced Judah *and his brothers.*" In verse 11 it says, "Josiah produced Jechoniah *and his brothers.*" The references encourage us to notice a link between the two. Jeannine Brown has pointed out that both refer to a period of time where the people are away from the land.[2] It was Judah and his brothers who migrated to Egypt (not expressly stated within the Matthean verse) while the next "and his brothers" occurred at the time of the forced migration to Babylon, which is expressly stated in verse 11.

If it is more than mere coincidence that both references correspond to a period of migration from the homeland and into foreign lands then we have another pattern. What would make it a stronger pattern would be a third example of a genealogical context in which a shift occurs into a horizontal line genealogy combined with a movement away from the land into foreign territory. The final unit in the final chapter of Matthew contains all these elements.

In Matt 28:18, Jesus has finally inherited "all authority in heaven and earth" and with this authority he sends out the eleven remaining men. The resurrected Jesus now refers to these men as his brothers (Matt 28:10). Jesus

---

2. "The repetition of the phrase 'and his brothers' highlights two important moments of the Old Testament story when Israel was away from the land promised to Abraham and his descendants." Brown, *Matthew,* 11.

tells the eleven men to go out into foreign lands discipling others (baptizing and teaching others what Jesus has taught them). In other words, the eleven "brothers" would be "reproducing" or extending the "lineage" not each by means of a vertical line production but by a horizontal branching out as they go out into non-Jewish territories. The movement is a kind of patrilateral (or "adelphi-lateral") branching out along with movement into foreign territories similar to what was seen in Matthew 1 ("and his brothers" in verses 2 and 11). The shift is from a vertical kind of inheritance (Matt 28:18) to a horizontal kind of inheritance whereby Jesus's "brothers" are extending the "lineage," branching out genealogically as well as geographically. Jesus is not simply the end of the line, the lineage now branches out horizontally from him.

Why the book of Matthew presents Jesus as teaching a group of men and why Jesus's teaching is targeting patriarchal issues are not separate questions. In order for the greater "kingdom" to arrive on earth the lesser "kingdom" must be dismantled. Human patriarchs must step down. The heavenly kingdom challenges would-be followers of the man Jesus to voluntarily dismantle their own patriarchal privileges and even to "emasculate themselves" by becoming like Eunuchs for the greater kingdom according to Matt 19:12 (εὐνούχισαν ἑαυτοὺς διὰ τὴν βασιλείαν τῶν οὐρανῶν).

Jesus does not ask the women to lower their status, only the free men. In Matthew, we do not find a modern western kind of feminism in which the women are raised up to have the same kind of powers and privileges as those possessed by the free men. Instead, there is a demoting of human patriarchy by challenging the desire for patriarchal powers and privileges.

If only such men could be less patriarchal by not striving to be bigger and gain more power and instead aim to become smaller and become less powerful—that would be a good place to start for those wanting to enable the greatest kingdom to arrive fully on earth—after all, that was what enabled the Messiah to arrive, according to Matthew 1.

Bibliography

Adelman, Rachel. "Seduction and Recognition in the Story of Judah and Tamar and the Book of Ruth." *Nashim: A Journal of Jewish Women's Studies & Gender Issues* 23 (2012) 87–109.

Anderson, Janice Capel. *Matthew's Narrative Web: Over, and Over, and Over Again.* Sheffield: JSOT, 1994.

Aquinas, Thomas. *Catena Aurea: Commentary on the Four Gospels, Collected out of the Works of the Fathers.* Vol. 1, London: John Henry Parker; J. G. F. and J. Rivington, 1842. https://ccel.org/ccel/aquinas/catena1/catena1.ii.i.html.

Ashmon, Scott A. *Birth Annunciations in the Hebrew Bible and Ancient near East: A Literary Analysis of the Forms and Functions of the Heavenly Foretelling of the Destiny of a Special Child.* Lewiston: Edwin Mellen, 2012.

Basil of Caesarea. "Homilia in sanctam Christi generationem." [On the Holy Nativity of Christ] Patrologia Graeca 31. Edited by J.-P. Migne. Paris: Migne, 1857.

Basser, Herbert. *The Mind Behind the Gospels: A Commentary to Matthew 1–14.* Boston: Academic Studies, 2009.

Boulding, Maria. *Expositions of the Psalms, 51–72.* Hyde Park: New City, 2001.

Boxall, Ian. *Discovering Matthew: Content, Interpretation, Reception.* London: SPCK, 2014.

Branch, Robin G. "When Mary Tells Joseph: A Play Based on Matthew 1:18–19." *In die Skriflig/In Luce Verbi* 47 (2013). 12 pages. https://doi.org/10.4102/ids.v47i1.92.

Brock, Sebastian P. *Treasure-House of Mysteries: Explorations of the Sacred Text through Poetry in the Syriac Tradition.* Yonkers: St. Vladimir's Seminary, 2012.

Brown, Jeannine K. *Matthew.* Teach the Text Commentary Series. Grand Rapids: Baker, 2015.

Carlson, Stephen C. "The Davidic Key for Counting the Generations in Matthew 1:17." *Catholic Biblical Quarterly* 76 (2014) 665–83.

Carter, Warren. *Matthew and the Margins: A Sociopolitical and Religious Reading.* Maryknoll: Orbis, 2000.

Chrysostom, John. "The Gospel of Matthew." Homily 4.3. In *Matthew 1–13,* edited by Manlio Simonetti and Thomas C. Oden, 12. Downers Grove: InterVarsity, 2001.

Classen, Carl Joachim. *Rhetorical Criticism of the New Testament.* Tübingen: Mohr Siebeck, 2000.

Clements, E. Anne. *Mothers on the Margin?: The Significance of Women in Matthew's Genealogy.* Eugene: Pickwick, 2014.

BIBLIOGRAPHY

Comfort, Philip Wesley. *New Testament Text and Translation Commentary: Commentary on the Variant Readings of the Ancient New Testament Manuscripts and How they Relate to the Major English Translations.* Carol Stream: Tyndale House, 2008.

Conway, Colleen M. *Behold the Man: Jesus and Greco-Roman Masculinity.* Oxford: Oxford University Press, 2008.

Davies, W. D., and Dale C. Allison, Jr. *A Critical and Exegetical Commentary on the Gospel According to Saint Matthew: Introduction and Commentary on Matthew I–VII.* Edinburgh: T. & T. Clark, 2007.

Do, Toan. *What Jesus Says about His Family: A Narrative and Semantic Reading.* Leiden: Brill, forthcoming. https://www.academia.edu/37157657.

Doane, Sébastien. "Masculinities of the Husbands in the Genealogy of Jesus (Matt. 1:2–16)." *Biblical Interpretation* 27 (2019) 91–106.

Duckwitz, Norbert H. O. *Reading the Gospel of St. Matthew in Greek: A Beginning, With Introduction, Notes, Vocabulary, and Grammatical Appendix.* Mundelein: Bolchazy-Carducci, 2014.

Evans, Craig A. "'The Book of the Genesis of Jesus Christ': The Purpose of Matthew in Light of the Incipit." In *Biblical Interpretation in Early Christian Gospels: Volume 2: The Gospel of Matthew*, edited by Thomas R. Hatina, 61–72. London: Bloomsbury T. & T. Clark, 2008.

———. *Matthew.* New Cambridge Bible Commentary. Cambridge: Cambridge University Press, 2012.

Fohrman, David. *Genesis: A Parsha Companion.* New Milford: Maggid, 2019.

France, R. T. *The Gospel of Matthew.* Grand Rapids: Eerdmans, 2007.

Gibson, Margaret Dunlop. *The Commentaries of Isho'dad of Merv Bishop of Ḥadatha (c. 850 A.D.).* Vol. 2, Matthew and Mark in Syriac. Cambridge: Cambridge University Press, 1911.

Hawk, Brandon W. *The Gospel of Pseudo-Matthew and the Nativity of Mary.* Eugene: Cascade, 2019.

Hamori, Esther J. "Heavenly Bodies: Pregnancy and Birth Omens in Israel." *Hebrew Bible and Ancient Israel* 2 (2013) 479–99.

Higgins, John B. "The Hidden Virtue of Women: Matthew 1." June 19, 2019. Video, 9:24. https://www.youtube.com/watch?v=HHXDKH_Scw4.

Hood, Jason B. *The Messiah, His Brothers, and the Nations: (Matthew 1.1–17).* London: Bloomsbury T. & T. Clark, 2011.

Holmes, Michael W. *Greek New Testament: SBL edition.* Atlanta: Society of Biblical Literature, 2010.

Howard, George. *Hebrew Gospel of Matthew.* Macon: Mercer University Press, 1995.

Kara-Ivanov Kaniel, Ruth. "The Myth of the Messianic Mother in Jewish and Christian Traditions: Psychoanalytic and Gender Perspectives." *Journal of the American Academy of Religion* 83 (2015) 72–119.

Kiraz, George Anton. *Comparative Edition of the Syriac Gospels: Aligning the Sinaiticus, Curetonianus, Peshîṭta and Ḥarklean Versions.* Vol. 1, 3rd ed. Piscataway: Gorgias, 2004.

Kitchen, Merrill. "Another Exile: 'Jesus and His Brothers' in the Gospel of Matthew." *Australian Biblical Review* 59 (2011) 1–12.

Klip, Hedda. *Biblical Genealogies: A Form-Critical Analysis, with a Special Focus on Women.* Leiden: Brill, 2022.

Lachs, Samuel Tobias. *A Rabbinic Commentary on the New Testament: The Gospels of Matthew, Mark, and Luke.* Hoboken: KTAV, 1987.

Levine, Amy-Jill. "Matthew." In *Women's Bible Commentary*, edited by Carol A. Newsom and Sharon H. Ringe, 339–49. Expanded edition; Louisville: Westminster John Knox, 1998.

———. "Women's Humor and Other Creative Juices," In *Are We Amused? Humour About Women In the Biblical World*, edited by Athalya Brenner, 120–26. London: Continuum T. & T. Clark International, 2003.

Lincoln, Andrew T. *Born of a Virgin?: Reconceiving Jesus in the Bible, Tradition, and Theology.* Grand Rapids: Eerdmans, 2013.

Loader, William. *The New Testament on Sexuality.* Grand Rapids: Eerdmans, 2012.

Mackie, Timothy, and Jonathan Collins. "Design Patterns in the Bible." March 30, 2018. Video, 6:06. https://www.youtube.com/watch?v=rkqsQpck8YU.

Miller, Robert J. "The Illegitimacy of Jesus in the Gospel of Matthew." *Juanita Voices* 8 (2008) 24–36.

Moore, Stephen D., and Janice Capel Anderson. "Matthew and Masculinity." In *New Testament Masculinities*, edited by Stephen D. Moore and Janice Capel Anderson, 67–91. Atlanta: Society of Biblical Literature, 2003.

Naseri, Christopher Naseri-Mutiti. "The Four OT Women in Matthew's Genealogy of Jesus," *Koinonia Journal* 5 (2011) 1–22.

Nolland, John. *The Gospel of Matthew: A Commentary on the Greek Text.* Grand Rapids: Eerdmans, 2005.

———. "No Son-of-God Christology in Matthew 1.18–25." *Journal for the Study of the New Testament* 62 (1996) 3–12.

O'Donnell, Matthew Brook, Stanley E. Porter, Jeffrey T. Reed, Robert Picirilli, Catherine J. Smith, and Randall K. Tan, eds. "Clause Level Annotation Specification." July 7, 2004. http://opentext.org/model/guidelines/clause/o-2.html.

Rahlfs, Alfred, and Robert Hanhart. *Septuaginta: SESB Edition.* Stuttgart: Deutsche Bibelgesellschaft, 2006.

Remaud, Michel. "Les femmes dans la généalogie de Jésus selon Matthieu." [Women in the genealogy of Jesus according to Matthew] *Nouvelle revue théologique* 143 (2021) 3–14.

Resseguie, James L. *Narrative Criticism of the New Testament: An Introduction.* Grand Rapids: Baker Academic, 2005.

Richter, Amy E. *Enoch and the Gospel of Matthew.* Eugene: Pickwick, 2012.

Satlow, Michael L. "A Detached Kiddushin." March 14, 2016. https://thegemara.com/article/a-detached-kiddushin.

Schaberg, Jane. "Feminist Interpretations of the Infancy Narrative of Matthew." In *A Feminist Companion to Mariology*, edited by Amy-Jill Levine with Maria Mayo Robbins, 15–36. London: Continuum T. & T. Clark International, 2005.

Schatkin, Margaret A. "The Perpetual Virginity of Mary and New Testament Criticism." In *De Maria Numquam Satis: The Significance of the Catholic Doctrines of the Blessed Virgin Mary for All People*, edited by Judith Marie Gentle and Robert L. Fastiggi, 37–67. Lanham: University Press of America, 2009.

Schweizer, Eduard. *The Good News According To Matthew.* Translated by David E. Green. Atlanta: John Knox, 1975.

Scott, Bernard Brandon. "The Birth of the Reader." *Semeia* 52 (1991) 83–102.

Scott, James M. *On Earth as in Heaven: The Restoration of Sacred Time and Sacred Space in the Book of Jubilees*. Leiden: Brill, 2005.

Smith, Mitzi J. "Fashioning Our Own Souls: A Womanist Reading of the Virgin-Whore Binary in Matthew and Revelation." In *I Found God in Me: A Womanist Biblical Hermeneutics Reader*, edited by Mitzi J. Smith, 158–82. Eugene: Cascade, 2015.

Soloveitchik, Elijah Zvi. *The Bible the Talmud, and the New Testament: Elijah Zvi Soloveitchik's Commentary to the Gospels*. Philadelphia: University of Pennsylvania Press, 2019.

Spencer, F. Scott. "Those Riotous—Yet Righteous—Foremothers of Jesus: Exploring Matthew's Comic Genealogy." In *Are We Amused? Humour About Women In the Biblical World*, edited by Athalya Brenner, 7–30. London: Continuum T. & T. Clark International, 2003.

Stendahl, Krister. "Quis et Unde—Who and Whence? Matthew's Christmas Gospel." In *Meanings: The Bible as Document and as Guide*, 71–83. Philadelphia: Fortress, 1984.

Swanson, Reuben J. *New Testament Greek Manuscripts: Matthew*. Sheffield: Sheffield Academic 1995.

Tarán, Leonardo, and Dimitri Gutas. *Aristotle Poetics: Editio Maior of the Greek Text with Historical Introductions and Philological Commentaries*. Leiden: Brill, 2012.

Viljoen, Francois P. "A Contextualised Reading of Matthew 6:22–23: 'Your eye is the lamp of your body.'" *HTS Theological Studies* 65 (2009). 5 pages. https://hts.org.za/index.php/hts/article/view/152/274.

Waetjen, Herman C. *The Origin and Destiny of Humanness: An Interpretation of the Gospel According to Matthew*. San Rafael: Crystal, 1975.

Wainwright, Elaine Mary. *Towards a Feminist Critical Reading of the Gospel According to Matthew*. Berlin: Walter de Gruyter, 1991.

———, Elaine. "Rachel Weeping for Her Children: Intertextuality and the Biblical Testaments—A Feminist Approach," In *A Feminist Companion to Reading the Bible: Approaches, Methods and Strategies*, edited by Athalya Brenner and Carole Fontaine, 425–70. London: Routledge, 2013.

Warner, Megan. "Uncertain Women: Sexual Irregularity and the Greater Righteousness in Matthew 1." *Pacifica* 18 (2005) 18–32.

Weren, Wim J. C. *Studies in Matthew's Gospel: Literary Design, Intertextuality, and Social Setting*. Leiden: Brill, 2014.

Yamasaki, Gary. *Perspective Criticism: Point of View and Evaluative Guidance in Biblical Narrative*. Eugene: Cascade, 2013.

Zaas, Peter. "Matthew's Birth Story: An Early Milepost in the History of Jewish Marriage Law." *Biblical Theology Bulletin* 39 (2009) 125–28.